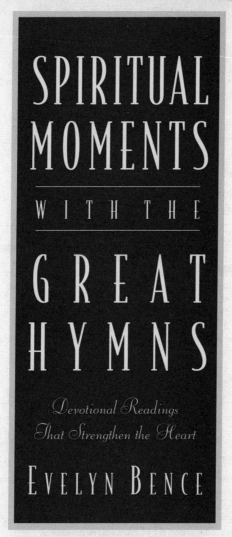

SPIRITUAL MOMENTS

WITH THE

GREAT HYMNS

Devotional Readings
That Strengthen the Heart

EVELYN BENCE

Illustrations by David Connell

ZondervanPublishingHouse
Grand Rapids, Michigan

A Division of HarperCollinsPublishers

Spiritual Moments with the Great Hymns
Copyright © 1997 by Evelyn Bence

Requests for information should be addressed to:

⛪ZondervanPublishingHouse
Grand Rapids, Michigan 49530

Library of Congress Cataloging-in-Publication Data

Bence, Evelyn, 1952–
   Spiritual moments with the great hymns : devotional readings that
strengthen the heart / Evelyn Bence.
      p. cm.
   Includes bibliographical references and index.
   ISBN: 0-310-20840-8 (alk. paper)
    1. Hymns—Devotional use.   2. Hymns, English—History and criticism.
I. Title.
BV340.B45 1997
264'.23—DC210

96-39869
CIP

Interior design by Jody A. DeNeef
Illustrations by David Connell

Printed in the United States of America

---

99 00 01 02 03 04 /❖ DC/ 10 9 8 7 6 5 4

For the Dear Ones —
still marching upward to Zion,
still singing the great songs

Acknowledgments

Thank you—

To the many friends and acquaintances who graciously told me their hymn-related epiphanies. Some of their stories are included in these pages. Others did not find their niche here. But I have valued them all and thank you for sharing a piece of your life with me.

Thank you—

To Ann Spangler for convincing me that this was a book I wanted to write.

To Bob Hudson for polishing my prose and cheering my efforts.

Contents

Part VI: Words That Challenge

Part VII: Hymns as Prayers

Part VIII: Songs of Testimony

Introduction

Would you have your songs endure?
Build on the human heart.

—Robert Browning

No really great song can ever attain full purport till long
after the death of its [original] singer, till it has accrued and
incorporated the many passions, many joys and sorrows, it
has itself aroused.

—Walt Whitman, *The Bible as Poetry*

Speak to one another with psalms, hymns and spiritual
songs. Sing and make music in your heart to the Lord,
always giving thanks to God the Father for everything, in
the name of our Lord Jesus Christ.

—Ephesians 5:19–20

My friend Jan remembers a conversation she had thirty
years ago in a small-town dentist's waiting room. Old Mrs. Gibbs
walked in and brought up the subject heavy on her mind: "I hate
coming to the dentist," she said.

Junior high Jan understood the sentiment.

"But," continued Mrs. Gibbs, "I sit in the chair and sing
hymns to myself. And I have no pain."

Jan was impressed with the power of the old praises and
promises. And so am I.

Jane Campbell, a coauthor of the popular book *Growing Up Born Again,* calls those hymns "our deposit"—valuable reserves hidden away for us to draw on. I like her phrase. We who were brought up in the church can recall the lines of poetry we learned effortlessly because they were set to memorable though not always meritorious music.

They're there, hidden in our hearts alongside King James Bible verses, for us to draw on in times of trouble; they surface in our minds when we sit in our houses, when we walk by the way, when we lie down, when we rise up.

I think I value these all the more in recent years since the church has lost its communal biblical language: the King James Version. Speaking of his Minnesota childhood, Garrison Keillor notes: "God spoke to us through his Word. Not in pictures, but in the King James Version, which was an everyday part of my life."[1] As much as I appreciate the contemporary, easier-to-read Bible translations for their ability to reach a new generation of readers, I mourn the breaking of the bond believers had when we all read and recited one set of matching Bible words. (Is this loss of an "authorized version" one key factor in the downfall of Scripture memorization? When I learn one version of John 3:16 in Sunday school and read it another way in my at-home Bible, do I master either?)

I propose that this loss of a common biblical language makes our heritage of song doubly important to the Christian community. Our songs, whether old or new, we can still sing and recite together as a group.

And many of our songs *are* new. Church music has changed dramatically in the last twenty years. Many old hymns or gospel favorites do not make their way onto overhead transparencies or the latest, revised hymnbooks.

At a recent Sunday school "assembly" (what we once called "opening exercises"), the superintendent asked soloists to sing old songs, including "He's the Lily of the Valley." Afterward church members came up, wondering where to find "that new song."

The superintendent was bemused. "That song? It's so old, it's new."

As a new generation of Christians caches away a new deposit of contemporary songs, I trust they will also rediscover some of the old greats. I smiled to hear that an annual informal gathering of charismatic leaders schedules what they call "roots night," on which they belt out hymns and gospel songs that are so old that, well, you might think them new. While those leaders have eagerly embraced the fresh, they also hold a deep appreciation for the old-but-not-necessarily-stale expressions of comfort and joy.

Whether you know old or new faith-songs, or neither, I trust you will find your faith renewed in the devotional stories and reflections in this book. I have asked many people to tell me their stories: *How and when did a particular hymn touch your spirit?* Many have a quick answer: *Oh, yes, I remember when . . .* It may be just one line of the song, but they can recall a precise moment when God's Spirit quickened a poet's phrase, penetrating, like the Scriptures themselves, "even to dividing . . . joints and marrow" (Hebrews 4:12). Many of these devotional readings recount a song's origins or offer a glimpse into the life of the woman or man who wrote the hymn. All of the readings lead you to consider God's word to you as you face daily victories, setbacks, challenges, and choices.

A few months before starting this book I read a moving article in the *New York Times Magazine,* in which Mary Gordon, a renowned Catholic novelist, painfully recounted scenes of her mother's once-vibrant life, now shrouded in senility. Mary had recently accompanied her mother as she received a disconcerting MRI test. When the older woman started thrashing in the machine, a nurse responded with harsh rebukes. Mary took another tack, yelling into the tunnel, "We're going to say the

Rosary." Mary's mother had lost most of her memory, and yet she, and Mary, recited the long litany, the words soothing her spirit.

Mary's reflection turned personal and it caught me up short. Mary suddenly saw that her mother possessed something Mary lacked and wished for: ". . . words that could automatically take away my terror. . . . [N]o passages . . . could be shouted at me and cause me to lie still."[2]

For a brief second I identified with Mary's personal assessment, struck voiceless in the face of terror. But I quickly knew I did have a ready word—in my hymn "deposit." Not one particular hymn but any one of the hundreds we sang in church (twice on Sunday, once midweek), on winter evenings around the piano, at summer camp meeting, in the car between home and "there yet," even climbing the stairs to go to bed. ("We're Marching to Zion" worked on us. You parents might try it.)

I still sing the songs of the saints of God. Old ones. New ones. With joy. Through tears. In hope. As Nelle Vander Ark notes, "Such a storehouse of song has been a reservoir of 'strength for today and bright hope for tomorrow'—often used by the Spirit to carry me through times of crisis."[3]

And now I offer this written song-based contribution to the community with the expectation that, as Walt Whitman said, "the strongest and sweetest songs yet remain to be sung." And those I'll learn at the feet of our Lord, the God musically addressed in Israel's very first poem: "I will sing to the LORD. . . . The LORD is my strength and my song" (Exodus 15:1–2).

E. B.
January 1997

Part I

Gifts of God

O worship the King, all-glorious above;
O gratefully sing his power and his love.
Sir Robert Grant

O the Deep, Deep Love of Jesus

Samuel Trevor Francis, 1834 - 1925

O the deep, deep love of Jesus,
Vast, unmeasured, boundless, free;
Rolling as a mighty ocean
In its fullness over me.
Underneath me, all around me,
Is the current of thy love;

As teenagers my older siblings gathered around the piano late on Sunday afternoons. They would leaf through the hymnal, picking out favorites to sing. In time, when I was welcomed into the group, I often requested "O the Deep, Deep Love" by Samuel Trevor Francis, a London merchant.

This was years before I'd seen the surf or fallen asleep on a beach, lulled by the ocean's forever rhythm. Even so, I could almost imagine the scene so clearly evoked by the song's rolling melody and deep bass line. The tune we sang is called *Ton-y-Botel,* based on a seemingly fictitious tale that the music was found in a bottle washed ashore in Wales.

O the deep, deep love of Jesus,
Spread his praise from shore to shore;
How he loveth, ever loveth,
Changeth never, never more. . . .

Today I write on a beach, mesmerized by the oceanic proportions of the love of God. A number of songwriters have worked with the theme. There's the folk line "I've got love like an ocean in my soul." There's the haunting verse of "The Love of God": If the oceans were filled with ink . . . "To write the love of God on high / Would drain the oceans dry."

Why have poets chosen oceans—not rivers or rocks—to grasp the grandeur of love?

The water before me is vast like Siberia. Deep like inverted Himalayas. Constant like tundra. Has this tide moved in and out and this surf pounded rhythmically since the days of creation?

And yet this water is a moving force as unpredictable as the wind that churns it, a body beyond the bounds of Adam's dominion.

The love of God, beyond comprehension, is poetically described in the most grand, wild way imaginable to a nineteenth-century writer. How else could one describe the indescribable: "How wide and long and high and deep is the love of Christ, . . . this love that surpasses knowledge" (Ephesians 3:18–19)?

For three days I have been staring at and listening to the rolling Atlantic, but I have watched from a distance—stayed on dry sand. Though I'm wearing a sundress, not bathing attire, I know I can sit here and observe no longer. It's time to hike up my skirt. Walk into the water. Let the waves lap at my legs as I raise the prayer of yet another hymn writer, W. D. Cornell. May it be your prayer as well:

> *Sweep over my spirit forever I pray*
> *In fathomless billows of love.*

Lord, your love may "surpass knowledge" but it does not bypass our human experience. Allow me to grasp its width and height and depth. In love and with love, sweep over my spirit, forever, starting today.

Great Is Thy Faithfulness

Thomas Chisholm, 1877 – 1957

Great is thy faithfulness!
Great is thy faithfulness!
Morning by morning new mercies I see;
All I have needed thy hand hath provided,
Great is thy faithfulness, Lord, unto me!†

Retired in sunny Florida, Bob Lytle, veteran mission-ary, lustily sings this hymn as his life theme.

The text was inspired by pivotal lines of Jeremiah's Lamentations. After a long litany of disaster and woe, Jeremiah gives a reason for hope: God is faithful and his compassions are new every morning.

Bob Lytle recalls the day when Chisholm's hymn and Jeremiah's point was indelibly stamped on his consciousness. It was 1945, the year he and his wife, Louise, and infant son left New York State for their first missionary tour.

The Lytles flew to Colombia, but they couldn't board with much baggage, being restricted to sixty pounds for each paying passenger. And most of that allotment, Bob says, "was claimed by diapers and baby necessities. Mom and Pop had lit-tle room for their clothing and household articles"—including

---

many items unavailable in the Third World. Bob and Louise packed all but the bare essentials for shipment by sea. They were told to expect the boxes and barrels to arrive at their door in three weeks.

In Medellin the Lytles moved into a mission apartment outfitted with basic furnishings. But weeks, then months, passed, and Bob started to wonder if the slow boat had sailed to Calcutta. He recalls, "Our son lived comfortably with plenty of diapers and rompers. But the parents—we watched our insufficient clothing become damaged, worn out, and detested. We longed for the useful gadgets" packed away and gone only God knew where.

Bob and Louise prayed for God's merciful will, and finally, *six months* later, the unaccompanied baggage arrived on two rickety, two-wheeled, horse-drawn flatbeds. Though battered, it had survived its sea voyage, the sun-baked docks, the customs inspection, and the train trip up the Andes from the coast.

The morning those tired horses stopped in the street, "it happened—no, God ruled it—that a fellow missionary in a neighboring apartment was playing 'Great Is Thy Faithfulness' on her vibraharp." Bob remembers the moment: "My spirit rose with that song as I thought how good, how faithful God had been. In hindsight, I see that the cartons may have contained only a few trinkets, but he had brought them in blessing to us."

Bob sees God's faithfulness not only in "providing" the long-delayed possessions but also in the timing of a neighbor's song of praise. "It was more than a fortuitous happening," he says of the music vibrating through the thin walls. It was God's not-so-subtle reminder—strong enough to last a lifetime— that he is *Jehovah-jireh,* the God Who Sees and the God Whose Provision Shall Be Seen. That event has been followed by uncounted encores, daily blessings, small and large, that reinforce this lesson learned as a young man.

And yet there have been days, weeks, when Bob could have written his own litany of lamentations. And that's when he chooses to take Jeremiah's tack—relying on recollection of previously acquired knowledge and understanding: "This I recall to mind, therefore I have hope."

As you face a new morning, recount God's faithfulness. Recollect his mercies. Recall the small and large miracles of your life. The material provisions. The orchestrated interventions. The reasons for your hope (Jeremiah 3:21 KJV).

Lord, when my hope and faith falter, remind me of specific times when I have been keenly aware of your faithful love and provision.

Like a River Glorious

Frances Ridley Havergal, 1836 – 78

Like a river glorious
Is God's perfect peace
Over all victorious
In its bright increase.

We are most aware of inner peace—its presence or its lack—in the midst of trial.

I expect that was true for Frances Ridley Havergal. A prolific British hymn writer, Havergal created poetic texts for the glory of God, but she also saw writing as her profession and livelihood. With great hopes of reaching a new market, she had signed a contract with an American publisher, but in January 1874 she received devastating news:

> I was expecting a letter from America, enclosing the 35 pounds now due me, and possibly news that "Bruey" was going on like steam, and "Under the Surface" pressingly wanted. The letter has come, and instead of all this, my publisher has failed in the universal crash. He holds my written promise to publish *only* with him as the condition of his launching me; so this is not simply a little loss, but an end of all my American prospects of either cash, influence, or fame, at any rate for a long time to come.

Months later, another publishing reversal: a printer's fire destroyed the only copy of a Havergal manuscript. She assessed the loss as a "winter's labor" of which she had "not even a memorandum left, having sent everything to the printers."

There may be no *direct* connection between one or both setbacks and the 1874 writing of "Like a river glorious / Is God's perfect peace." But I suggest the link. After all, every event or experience *is* food for a writer's imagination. Besides, aren't we most conscious of peace when we walk through chaos?

Havergal's underlying "peace like a river" image is biblical, appearing several times in the prophecies of Isaiah. I find one reference particularly interesting, as it is directly preceded by a description of God teaching his children the road to the riverbank. Here's the complete picture:

> I am the LORD your God,
>> who teaches you what is best for you,
>> who directs you in the way you should go.
> If only you had paid attention to my commands,
>> your peace would have been like a river.
>
> Isaiah 48:17 - 18

Did Havergal find peace in the midst of her trials? Yes. Her account of the failed American publisher continues: "Two months ago this would have been a real trial to me, for I had built a good deal on my American prospects: now 'Thy will be done' is not a sigh [a personal pain], but only a *song!*"

And here's her take on the manuscript destroyed in the fire: "It may be that [God] has more to teach me. . . . He is giving me the opportunity *over again* of doing [the work] more patiently, and of making it the 'willing service' which I don't think it was before."

Here is a woman well on her way to "perfect peace"—what the Hebrews called "shalom shalom"—peace to the second degree. Isaiah 26:3 gives the promise: "You [God] will keep in perfect peace / him whose mind is steadfast, / because he trusts in you." The peace is discovered, as Havergal found, as one learns to be

> *Stayed upon Jehovah, [where]*
> *Hearts are fully blest;*
> *Finding as he promised,*
> *Perfect peace and rest.*

Like Havergal, you and I may have more lessons to learn before we find the perfect peace that stills a heart in the midst of chaos or loss. But today we can take one step—choosing to stay our hearts and minds upon Jehovah, turn our eyes upon Jesus, the Prince of Peace.

Lord, in the midst of trial, loss, and chaos, allow me to know the peace that transcends understanding. If that peace comes only as I learn to heed your lessons, then make me teachable. Help me learn to turn to you, the Prince of Peace, to discover what peace means.

Amazing Grace

John Newton, 1725 - 1807

Amazing grace! how sweet the sound
That saved a wretch like me!
I once was lost, but now am found,
Was blind but now I see.

Aging baby boomers have claimed "Amazing Grace" as their unofficial anthem. This favor is a recent phenomenon. A 1950 hymnology textbook, for instance, gave six pages to the life and work of hymn writer John Newton but never mentioned his autobiographical "Amazing Grace." In 1975 Joan Baez urged her audience to join her as she sang the "traditional" song; to make things easy, she lined out the verses, giving the words phrase by phrase, even for the first verse. These days that's no longer necessary; on tour, Judy Collins ends her concerts with this very song—knowing full well that her audience will join in without needing cues from the stage. The hymn was even featured at President Clinton's second inaugural ceremony.

Why has a song about the conversion of a "wretch like me"—about being lost then found, blind then sighted—captured the heart of a generation that deems itself too enlightened to use the word *sin?* (One congregation asks God to forgive them their "negativity.")

Part of the song's enchantment is its oft-told history. Folksingers, Christian musicians, evangelists, even Bill Moyers on public television—all have sketched Newton's dramatic spiritual transformation: God plucked a young degenerate slave-ship captain from a profane profession and set him on an exemplary path.

In midlife Newton was ordained an Anglican priest; he was an acclaimed hymn writer, and in his older years he influenced the political movement that would abolish the slave trade in the British Empire. It's the story cryptically told in "Amazing Grace," published when Newton was fifty-four:

> *'Tis grace that brought me safe thus far,*
> *And grace will lead me home.*

Newton's testimony kindles promise in aging idealists. If Newton could be transformed, there's hope for us. Not that we see ourselves as wretched as he (few of us admit the depths of our own depravity), but then we *haven't* ever been able to locate and "get ourselves back to the garden." On the whole, the negativity remains. At middle age we can see that even our best intentions have caused harm, been skewed, gone awry. We're in trouble—still—and we need help.

As a generational group we sense our need for grace—sustaining if not saving—and yet we are very grateful for the lot of it we've preveniently received. We never really believed that crawling under a school desk would protect us from any manner of missile. We hardly dared hope we'd ever be grandparents. But here we are, survivors—thanks to the amazing grace that has seen us through these many dangers, toils, and snares.

Previous generations have claimed other hymns as period anthems, notably songs challenging people to fight for a cause: "Mine Eyes Have Seen the Glory" for Union sympathizers in the Civil War; "Onward Christian Soldiers" for Theodore Roosevelt campaign supporters and Allied soldiers in World War I.

And today, with a tentative truce in a long Cold War, a generation looks for a spiritual truce, a grace and peace that will carry them across a millennial divide. As they sing for grace, may they find John Newton's life-changing God.[†]

At age eighty-two, facing life's greatest transition, Newton was still singing his graceful theme; just months before he died, he said, "My memory is nearly gone, but I remember two things, that I am a great sinner, and that Christ is a great Savior."

And maybe in time—who knows?—baby boomers will grasp these same two things.

He will my shield and portion be
As long as life endures.

─────────

*L*ord, make me aware of my sin. Make me equally aware of your amazing grace—the everyday graces of life and the grace of salvation.

[†]See "May the Grace of Christ Our Savior" on page 215 for more insight into Newton's life.

As Pants the Hart

Nahum Tate, 1652 – 1715, and Nicholas Brady, 1659 – 1726

As pants the hart for cooling streams
When heated in the chase,
So longs my soul, O God, for thee,
And thy refreshing grace.

Years ago I noticed in print a misquoted Psalm 42:1. In the King James Version the verse reads, "As the hart panteth after the water brooks, so panteth my soul after thee, O God." Not realizing that *hart* is an outdated word for *deer*, the writer had typed, "As the heart panteth after the water...." The editor in me cringed at the mistake; it made the Bible verse redundant at best, at worst, nonsensical. But the more I thought about it, the more tolerant I grew. On some ethereal plane, the skewed connection was understandable; it maybe even worked. The English language provides a tidy play on words. The hart and heart are thirsty.

As staid as it now seems, singing the Nahum Tate and Nicholas Brady paraphrase of Psalm 42 was too revolutionary for some British churchmen of the late seventeenth century who held to a long-standing prohibition of congregational singing of any songs but strictly translated psalms. They disapproved, for instance, of the heated hunter's *chase* in line 2 that draws out one's imagination; this is a capital-letter thirst.

Poets ancient and modern have recognized the power of the image: "I'm thirsty."

In her poem "The Prayer," Sharon Olds lays out a capital-letter scene. A young girl sits in a veterinarian's waiting room. Behind a closed door, her sick pet gerbils are being "put to sleep." The poem portrays subtle signs of distress; the girl doesn't cry; she doesn't talk about her gerbils, her loss, her first encounter with death; she doesn't name her feelings; she quietly repeats only one phrase: "I'm thirsty. I'm thirsty," as if her sun-dried soul were panting, praying, for the water of life.[1]

Psalm 42 itself does not promise the clear, flowing streams that will rehydrate the sin-dried soul. But Jesus picked up on the image when speaking to a woman drawing water from a well at his request: "If you knew the gift of God and who it is that asks you for a drink, you would have asked him and he would have given you living water" (John 4:10). *If you knew what God offers, you would ask for a drink. You would gasp, "I'm thirsty. God, my soul pants for you."*

Isaiah 44:3 also promises fulfillment for the soul who longs for God. Lucy Rider paraphrases the verse:

> *I [God] will pour water on him who is thirsty,*
> *I will pour floods upon the dry ground.*

And then she adds a personal invitation reminiscent of Jesus' in John 4; here's how to ask for the gift of living water:

> *Open your heart for the gift I am bringing,*
> *While ye are seeking me, I will be found.*

The eternal God offers the refreshing drink. Ask and receive. Take and drink.

Lord, you have promised to quench the thirst of those who turn to you and ask you for living water. I'm thirsty. Fill my cup, please, and I will drink.

O Sacred Head Now Wounded

Bernard of Clairvaux, 1091 - 1153
trans. and verse 4 added by
James Waddell Alexander, 1804 - 59

What language shall I borrow
To thank thee, dearest Friend,
For this thy dying sorrow,
Thy pity without end?

Before I knew her, Maggie worked in the theater: teaching, acting, directing, producing. But somewhere on the West Coast, the talent fogged in. Giving a dramatic reading in front of a collége class, she stopped cold, overwhelmed with unexplainable panic.

That attack spawned others until fear pervaded her life. As for her career, when I met Maggie, she worked as a secretarial temp. She hadn't performed for four years, grounded by the terror of feeling out of control. As for her personal life, she drove little—went to great lengths to avoid bridges or interstates. And escalators—they might as well have been mountain cliffs.

The fear held on for nearly ten years before it lost its grip. Maggie made a few bold ventures up and down a shopping-mall escalator, driving over a bridge. She celebrated a few small victories. And then God broke through with the words of a song often sung during Holy Week, "O Sacred Head Now Wounded." Most of the words are attributed to Bernard of Clairvaux, a medieval saint. But the fourth verse is comparatively new, written in 1830 by James Waddell Alexander, a Presbyterian pastor in Trenton, New Jersey. For Maggie, that "addition," sung by her congregation one Sunday in Lent, was the clincher—and the clench-releaser.

"What language shall I borrow?" The line spoke to the magnitude of Maggie's need, which she saw as being beyond description in her own language. She found it impossible to articulate the paralysis brought on by a panic attack.

The line also helped her lay claim to the knowledge that God is beyond words. "His love and grace is indescribable— and greater than my confusion," she says. More than that, it helped her reach a new *gratitude* for the ability to make small steps toward recovery.

Several weeks ago I went to a movie with Maggie—and she was the one assuring *me* that I was not likely to trip down the escalator and break my skull. And she's back teaching college students the secrets of public speaking.

"But," she admits, "I still can't sing that verse without choking up."

Sometimes, still, the fear does creep in. When that happens the hymn's last phrases kick in and Maggie keeps moving— beyond the panic to the peace:

> Oh, make me thine forever!
> And should I fainting be,
> Lord, let me never, never,
> Outlive my love for thee.

Lord, your Word assures us that your Spirit will help us in our weakness. When I do not know how to pray, intercede for me with that language that is beyond human utterance. Accept the groanings of my heart—its depravity and its gratitude for your grace.

We Plow the Fields, and Scatter

Matthias Claudius, 1740 – 1815
trans. by Jane Campbell, 1817 – 78

We plow the fields, and scatter
    The good seed on the land,
But it is fed and watered
    By God's almighty hand.

*I*t's a few years after the American Revolution. But not on the western side of the Atlantic. In Germany, north of Frankfurt. Matthias Claudius, provincial commissioner of Agriculture and Manufactures, is also a man of letters who writes a long play titled *Paul Erdmann's Feast*. It's a harvest tale, culminating in neighborhood jubilation as the last wagon-load of produce is drawn in from the fields. Paul Erdmann's celebration starts not with firecrackers but with the singing of a "Peasant Song"—seventeen four-line verses, each sung as a solo, each ending with "all" joining in on the chorus:

All good gifts around us
    Are sent from heaven above;
Then thank the Lord, O thank the Lord,
    For all his love.

Six worthy verses of the "Peasant Song"—loosely translated and paired to make three song stanzas—have landed in our hymnals. But with each passing year, I fear, the song inches its way toward oblivion. The closest most of us get to fresh fields is the supermarket produce department. And what do we know about scattering seeds?

In his refreshing *The Book of Hymns,* Ian Bradley quotes an "anonymous" revised version:

> *We plough the fields with tractors*
> *With drills we sow the land.*
> *But growth is still the wondrous gift*
> *Of God's almighty hand.*[2]

This song might be totally lost to a new generation if it had not been boldly repackaged for Broadway. The contemporary *Godspell* stage tune is difficult but strangely rewarding— like farmwork, if one can believe my father, who for some reason unbeknownst to me can recall with nostalgia the labor of steering a horse-drawn plow.

"We Plow the Fields" is now relegated to a narrow autumn slot—our Thanksgiving holiday—that harks back to the song's harvest origins. That's a perfect weekend to start expressing our thanks for all the "bright and good" harvests that may be hard-wrought but ultimately come to fruition only if God-graced with growth.

And yet Thanksgiving is no window of opportunity that slams shut with the advent of December.

All fifty-two weeks a year we can take a lesson from a *Godspell* disciple, named Lemar in the original production. In the stage musical, the song's age-old hymnal words remain intact. But as a belabored chorus fades out—"All good gifts around us / Are sent from heaven above"—one blessed man, Lemar, steps out of the crowd and bursts forth with a flamboyant "I really want to thank you, Lord."

As if he can't help himself. As if he had opened his arms and received a gift so expansive and wonderful he could think of only one appropriate response—that which God most desires: a "humble, thankful heart."

And we echo his refrain, "I really want to thank you, Lord."

* * *

Lord, in every arena of life it's easy for me to "plow" and then "harvest"—and then take all the credit for the crop, as if I had also provided the sun and the rain and worked the photosynthesis. Forgive me for neglecting to thank you privately and publicly for your good gifts. For your wonder-working power—in nature and in the human heart. Thank you. Yes, thank you.

Part II

Tidings of Christmas Joy

Sing, choirs of angels, sing in exultation,
Sing, all ye citizens of heaven above!
Glory to God, all glory in the highest;
O come, let us adore him,
Christ the Lord.

John Francis Wade

Silent Night

Joseph Mohr, 1792 – 1848

Silent night, holy night,
All is calm, all is bright;
Round yon virgin mother and child!
Holy Infant, so tender and mild,
Sleep in heavenly peace.

There are two versions of what happened on December 24, 1818, the day "Silent Night" ("Stille nacht") was "born" in the tiny village of Oberndorf, near Salzburg, Austria. The basic scene holds in both accounts. The Oberndorf Roman Catholic Church of Saint Nicholas had a new, young priest, Joseph Mohr.

Version 1 of the "Silent Night" story starts the evening of December 23, at an annual Christmas pageant presented by amateur actors from a neighboring town. The party was hosted by an Oberndorf businessman, who went out of his way to invite the new priest into the village celebration.

The warm welcome he received and the utterly primitive reenactment of the Christmas story deeply touched Mohr. Not ready for sleep after the celebration, he took a walk—up onto a hill overlooking Oberndorf. From the view—the wide scope of the dark sky, the lights of the village below—he drank the inspiration for a poem "Stille nacht, heilige nacht." He walked home and that night wrote out the verses.

The next morning, Christmas Eve, he gave the poem to the church organist, composer Franz Gruber, asking for music that would make it work. The tune came quickly; the church organ happened to be broken, so Gruber wrote his arrangement as a duet with guitar accompaniment. Why not sing it tonight?

They did. At the Christmas Eve mass, Mohr and Gruber introduced the song to the village.

The organ repairman (some say he was at the service; some say he came to the church later "on business") spread the song from village to village. Traveling folksingers picked up the song and spread it into Germany—and from there it needed little help making it around the world.

Version 2 of the story has a different focus. Here the poem was born of crisis. In this account Mohr was motivated by necessity as much as inspired by the nativity. On December 24 the organ broke, throwing the inexperienced twenty-six-year-old priest and the organist into high gear. As planned and practiced, the music for the Christmas Eve service fell apart if the organ fell silent. The service—the liturgical highlight of the winter—was in shambles. What to do now?

Mohr and Gruber quickly wrote a new song, which they sang as a duet with guitar accompaniment.

I'm not sure it matters which version is true—slow reflection or crash crisis. That December one way or another that memorable song was conceived in Joseph Mohr's heart. On paper and in performance Mohr and others saw evidence of its birth. And to this day the results of that birth remain. Does any song strike a truer chord on Christmas Eve? Christ the Savior is born.

Think in terms of any believer's spiritual birth—new life in Christ. Slow reflection (long incubation and gentle birth) or dramatic, emotional zap—does the circumstance of the birth matter as much as the evidence of it?

For purposes of this application, I say hang the particulars. Here's what matters: the Spirit rustled within Joseph Mohr, and a poem was born. He knew it. His coworker recognized it. His village heard it. A traveler spread witness of it. And in time the world was blessed by it.

The same can be said of the Spirit's work in you or me or our friends or neighbors. A dramatic event isn't evidence of a spiritual birth.

If you're looking for evidence of the Spirit's work in your life, look beyond the dramatic. Look for faith, look for godly fruit, look for "poems" worth repeating, and songs you can't keep from humming.

Lord, I give your Spirit permission to work in my heart and life as you see fit, whether that be in a crisis or dramatic situation or quietly. Allow me to see evidence of your work—evidence on your terms, not my own.

In the Bleak Midwinter

Christina Georgina Rossetti, 1830 - 94

In the bleak midwinter,
Frosty wind made moan,
Earth stood hard as iron,
Water like a stone;
Snow had fallen, snow on snow,
Snow on snow,
In the bleak midwinter, long ago.

I intended this morning to write about a children's song sung in Holy Week, "There is a green hill far away ... Where the dear Lord was crucified. . . ."

But the mood isn't right. The muse doesn't strike. It's hard for me to imagine what a green hill looks like.

I've been housebound now for a week, surrounded by snow on snow on snow. The steep road that runs between me and anywhere is slick with ice like a stone or maybe it's iron.

They're calling it the Blizzard of '96, and this act of God has shut down the federal government, the East Coast airports, and, briefly, Wall Street. A *Washington Post* columnist says about the only sane thing to do is to avoid "the company of people from Buffalo."[1]

I grew up and went to college near Buffalo, as did Becky Hutton, who loves Christina Rossetti's hymn for its "word pictures that made me feel and hear and see winter." The author's skill in "creating a mood delighted me. But," says Becky, "what I have come to appreciate even more is the awe of the second verse. Every time I hear it I feel as if I need to stop and kneel."

That second verse describes what happened in the chilly setting:

> Our God, heaven cannot hold him,
> Nor earth sustain;
> Heaven and earth shall flee away
> When he comes to reign;
> In the bleak midwinter
> A stable place sufficed
> The Lord God almighty, Jesus Christ.

Granted, in Bethlehem virtually any snow melts in a day. And most scholars doubt that the sufficient "stable place" sheltered the Christ child in the dead of winter. Rossetti was transporting a local English setting onto a biblical scene.

And yet a universal truth stands behind Rossetti's provincial lines. Christ came to earth in and for such a time as this: the blustery blizzards, the discontented winters.

In a poem titled "A Better Resurrection," Rossetti again uses *stone* as a hard simile.

> My heart within me like a stone
> Is numbed too much for hopes or fears. . . .
> O Jesus, quicken me.

This time the image is reminiscent of Ezekiel's prophecy: the Lord saying, "I will remove from them their heart of stone and give them a heart of flesh" (11:19). Warm. Pliable. Pulsating. He will take the stone—the iron, the ice—and replace it with life.

Rossetti in yet another poem claims: "Spring shall bloom where now the ice is."

Contemplating that promise—although I'm still looking out at a paralyzing snowstorm—I am suddenly able to envision a green Good Friday hill and an April Easter garden. Where an angel rolled a stone away. And death was turned to life.

If you're looking out over a frozen, wintry scene, leap ahead to the springtime thaw. Let the Christ warm your heart.

Lord, this song reminds me that you were willing to enter our winter—to usher us into the spring that your incarnation made possible. Jesus, quicken me. Bring your life, your warmth, to my cold, stony heart. Even now, in this bleak midwinter, open my sight to the promise of spring.

Once in Royal David's City

Cecil Frances Alexander, 1818 – 95

Once in royal David's city
Stood a lowly cattle shed,
Where a mother laid her baby
In a manger for his bed:
Mary was that mother mild,
Jesus Christ, her little child.

My Christmas holiday begins on December 24, when, through the wonders of radio, the first strains of "Once in Royal David's City" are beamed across the Atlantic, one clear line sung by a young boy, a first-year member of King's College Choir. Custom runs deep in Cambridge, England. Every year since 1919 the Christmas Eve Service of Nine Lessons and Carols has opened with the same word, "Once . . . ," intoned by a solitary child.

I understand there's another element of the tradition. *All* the eight-year-old choirboys are ready to sing that unaccompanied solo, the note awaited around the world. No one knows whom the choirmaster will choose—until it's time to queue up.

Everyone is prepared.

As was Mary, once in Nazareth.

As was the Son, once in heaven—at the appointed time ready and willing to become flesh and live among us.

> *He came down to earth from heaven,*
> *Who is God and Lord of all . . .*

> *With the poor and mean and lowly*
> *Lived on earth our Savior holy.*

As was Cecil Frances Alexander once in Ireland, who, in the words of the apostle, was "prepared to give an answer to everyone who asks . . . the reason for the hope" within her (1 Peter 3:15). I would emphasize *everyone,* because Alexander wrote some four hundred hymns or poems, nearly all of them attempts to explain the Christian faith to children in her Sunday school. An Anglican pastor's wife keenly aware of the liturgical calendar, she composed a poem for every Sunday of the year and all the holy days. She also wrote hymns that explicated the Apostles' Creed—for children, but with such eloquence that a number are still sung and appreciated by old and young alike. Such as "Once in Royal David's City," her elaboration of the creedal "I believe . . . / in Jesus Christ his only Son our Lord; / who was conceived by the Holy Ghost, / born of the Virgin Mary."

Once as a grown man, our Lord asked his disciples—of all generations, even ours—to *be prepared* to meet their Creator. "Keep watch," he said, "because you do not know the day or the hour" (Matthew 25:13).

When you will be "called home."

When Jesus—now returned to the Father in heaven—will come back to earth, this time to claim the redeemed. To judge the quick and the dead.

> *And our eyes at last shall see him,*
> *Through his own redeeming love;*
> *For that child so dear and gentle*
> *Is our Lord in heaven above,*

And he leads his children on
To the place where he is gone.

Are you prepared to follow?

Not in that poor lowly stable
*   With the oxen standing by*
We shall see him, but in heaven,
*   Set at God's right hand on high.*
Are you prepared for the meeting?

When like stars his children crowned
All in white shall wait around.

Are you prepared to sing your part?

Lord, I want to be ready to leave this world for your heavenly kingdom. Just as Mary was ready to receive your message and your Spirit—your first advent—help me prepare my heart. Come Lord Jesus. Come.

I Heard the Bells on Christmas Day

Henry Wadsworth Longfellow, 1807 – 82

I heard the bells on Christmas day
Their old familiar carols play,
And wild and sweet the words repeat
Of peace on earth, good will to men.

*T*wenty years ago I saw some cleverness in the title of a book by Francis Schaeffer: *He Is There and He Is Not Silent.* Now I think the line a poor imitation of Henry Wadsworth Longfellow's classic line from this classic carol: "God is not dead, nor doth he sleep."

A seasoned Longfellow wrote "I Heard the Bells" in the long, cold winter of 1863–64. This aging, popular poet knew the rush of success, his *Song of Hiawatha* selling a million copies in his lifetime. But he had also been agonizingly crushed with the loss of his wife, whose life had burned out when her gauzy dress accidentally ignited. And the War Between the States mercilessly raged. Longfellow was an ardent abolitionist, but the cost of war was high. Antietam. Vicksburg. Gettysburg. Sons, fathers, and brothers—from Maine to Mississippi, thousands had not come home for Christmas.

And yet . . . for such a winter as this, Christ had come to earth.

My younger brother connects "I Heard the Bells" with a bad-dream scenario related in the December 25 entry of *Streams in the Desert,* the dog-eared devotional by Mrs. Charles E. Cowman that reigned over the bathroom of our childhood.

In Mrs. Cowman's account, a pastor has a Christmas morning nightmare in which he views the world without Christ. He dreams that he is called to a woman's deathbed. He opens his Bible to offer comfort but finds no New Testament, no resurrection promises, no gospel consolation. In his dream he weeps bitterly, viewing a world without the Christmas Christ.

But suddenly the preacher wakes up, drawn back to the real world as he hears the strains of a familiar carol attesting the Lord's coming.

As Mrs. Cowman told the story, the breakthrough song was not Longfellow's "I Heard the Bells on Christmas Day." But try to tell my brother that.

"That pastor's nightmare has always haunted me," he says. "If Christ had not come, would there be any hope for our world? Even as it is, I shudder when I watch the evening news. Verse 3 of 'I Heard the Bells' summarizes my personal nightmare":

> And in despair I bowed my head:
> "There is no peace on earth," I said,
> "For hate is strong, and mocks the song
> Of peace on earth, good will to men."

"Verse 4 wakes me from my horrid dream."

> Then pealed the bells more loud and deep:
> "God is not dead, nor doth he sleep;
> The wrong shall fail, the right prevail,
> With peace on earth, good will to men."

Sometimes it is hard to grasp the angelic promise of ultimate peace—made by angels to Bethlehem shepherds: "Glory to God in the highest, and on earth peace, good will toward men." It speaks of a future day. Yet Christ himself declared that "the gates of hell" would "not prevail" against his church (Matthew 16:18 KJV). The wrong shall fail. The good shall triumph.

We may still anticipate that final celebration of victory, but we don't have to wait for the reality of Longfellow's memorable present-tense line: "God is not dead, nor doth he sleep."

Let the belfries roll the song. Christ has come. God is here and far from silent.

❧

Lord, whether it's Christmas Day or mid-July, throughout this day give me reminders of your presence here with me. Wake me out of my nightmares by allowing me to hear the songs of Zion.

O Little Town of Bethlehem

Phillips Brooks, 1835 – 93

O little town of Bethlehem,
How still we see thee lie!
Above thy deep and dreamless sleep
The silent stars go by;
Yet in thy dark streets shineth
The everlasting Light;
The hopes and fears of all the years
Are met in thee tonight.

I sometimes think I'm becoming obsessed with *aging*. I recently met a college friend I hadn't seen in seven years. I later talked to a mutual acquaintance. "Burnett's showing his age," I said, meaning, I hope I don't look as old as he does.

"We all are," she answered matter-of-factly.

Yes. There's the reality of my parents' shallow breath. My sisters' growing grandchildren. Memories of my once supple skin.

Such somber thoughts come to me more frequently in the dark days of winter, with the turning of the new year, with the mixed emotions—anticipation, joy, nostalgia, disappointment—that accompany Christmas.

And this winter I find my mind frequently returning to two lines of a Christmas carol that has been popular ever since it was first published in 1874. Some songs "make it" despite their tunes. (The British have found a wonderful melody, called "Forest Green.") For "O Little Town of Bethlehem," the *words* by Phillips Brooks—not a poet but a world-class preacher—speak. Brooks, who had previously spent a year in Palestine and a Christmas Eve on the hills above Bethlehem, penned the lines for a Philadelphia children's Sunday school program. As a thirty-three-year-old bachelor, did Brooks know how time can entangle hopes with fears and reduce years to decades? Did he know his gentle assurance would stir aging children hearing his lines a generation after he lies silent in the grave? "The hopes and fears of all the years / Are met in thee tonight."

All the hopes. Of an after-school playmate, of lifelong social security, of a band of angels to carry me home.

All the fears. Of the Lindbergh-baby kidnapper outside the window, of the debilitating winter chill, of the grim reaper at the bedside.

Are met—put to rest—in the Christ who came to Bethlehem.

When someone asked the secret of his life, a mature Brooks referred to a present reality that ushered him to a greater hope. His secret, he said, was

> a deeper knowledge and truer love of Christ.... He is here. He knows me and I know Him. It is no figure of speech. It is the realest thing in the world. And every day makes it realer, and one wonders with delight what it will grow to as the years go on.

If that was Brooks' life-secret, it doesn't surprise me that his favorite scriptural text was John 10:10, Jesus' addressing his own advent: "I am come that they might have life, and that they might have it more abundantly" (KJV).

They. The young. The middle-aged. The old. In summer. In winter. All. Take a deep breath. Breathe it in. Sing the song.

O holy child of Bethlehem!
Descend to us, we pray;
Cast out our sin, and enter in;
Be born in us today.

Angels We Have Heard on High

Traditional French Carol, nineteenth century

Angels we have heard on high
Sweetly singing o'er the plains,
And the mountains in reply
Echoing their joyous strains.
Gloria in excelsis Deo.

Glory to God in the highest and peace to his people on earth. Every Sunday liturgically minded Christians around the world repeat the line sung by angels in the company of shepherds abiding in Bethlehem fields. The first lines of "The Gloria," originally from Luke's account of the Christmas story, transcend the season. They draw together two worlds: God and humanity; heaven and earth. Like the Incarnation itself. Like the French carol: "Angels we have heard on high ... And the mountains in reply ... Gloria."

Not much is known about the origins of this French carol. It feels *old,* but it hasn't been found in written records earlier than 1855. A few years later it was translated into English and has gained popularity with recent generations.

With its repetitious, monotonous verse tune, the song might well have been lost to history—like its author—if not for its breakout refrain. Only a Scrooge can resist the joyous "Gloria in excelsis Deo." You can almost believe the angelic host was singing Latin words to Hebrew shepherds, drawing them to go see the Christ.

Three years ago, the Spirit used this carol to bridge two worlds for a cancer-wracked woman. At this stage of her life, a lot of details escaped Josephine Dayton; her mind was often fogged in, but she did know she was dying. At Thanksgiving she visited her daughter. Shortly before she left to return to the nursing home, two hours away, she lucidly announced, "This is the last time I'll be here."

"But it's only a month until Christmas," her daughter, Camilla, responded. "Surely you'll be coming for Christmas?"

This simple calendar calculation took Jo by surprise: "Oh?" She paused. "I guess I can wait that long."

In December, Camilla just once articulated the unthinkable: "Mom, I'm not sure we'll be able to get you home for Christmas." *You can hardly get out of bed.*

The look on Jo's face confirmed Camilla's suspicions: Christmas with the family was the one thing holding Jo here.

Despite warnings from the care-facility management *(we don't advise her leaving the premises; we won't be responsible; you'll have to sign papers; you'll have to keep her on oxygen the whole time)*, Camilla brought Jo home for Christmas. To the white-light tree. To a fireplace framed by a mantelpiece crowded with Camilla's collection of treasured Christmas angels. To tagged packages (four for Jo, including the latest twelve-month calendar annually illustrated and comprehensively numbered by her adolescent granddaughter). To the family feast (one portion pureed).

Midafternoon the hour approached, time for Jo to leave. As the car warmed up, Camilla asked her daughter to please play a piano piece for Grandma Jo. A carol. From her meager repertoire, she chose "Angels We Have Heard on High."

At the sound of the first bright chord, a hush fell over the house. Mesmerized by the music and the shimmering angel-topped tree, Jo sat perfectly still, her mind on the far side of some calm, wide river.

> *Come to Bethlehem and see*
> *Him whose birth the angels sing;*
> *Come, adore on bended knee*
> *Christ, the Lord, the newborn King.*

As the last note died out, Jo whispered, "That was beautiful." As if to say thank you. As if to say she'd been transported to another world.

Once back in her own bed, Jo lingered in this land, but only hours. The next morning she followed an angel bidding her to cross over: *Come and see . . . him of whom the angels sing. Come, adore on bended knee, Christ . . . Jesus the Lord of heaven and earth.*

You and I may not be as close to "the river bank" as was Jo when she heard her granddaughter play this French carol, and yet on any and every day we are invited—called—to sing the refrain that is carved into an ancient liturgy and a lively faith: *Glory to God in the highest.*

Sing it with the angels on high. And let the mountains echo your praise.

Lord, joining my voice with angels and archangels and with all the company of heaven, I sing a hymn of praise: Glory to God in the highest. Gloria in excelsis Deo.

We Three Kings

John Henry Hopkins, 1820 – 91

We three kings of Orient are,
Bearing gifts we traverse afar
Field and fountain, moor and mountain,
Following yonder star.

The *Oxford Book of Carols* says that the word *carol* "has a dancing origin." Carols, it explains, are "songs with a religious impulse that are simple, hilarious [joyful], popular, and [when written] modern ... rich in true folk-poetry." Some "ramble on like a ballad."

From the book's prosy definition of this song category, I see that carols are like good gifts: "generally spontaneous and direct in expression." Many mediocre carols are duly forgotten, but good carols "retain their vitality" because they are sincere; because they ring true in their own age, they hold their ground across time.[2]

Skimming through this classic Oxford collection, I am surprised that many of the joy-filled Christmas hymns aren't cataloged as carols: "O Little Town of Bethlehem," "O Come, All Ye Faithful," "Joy to the World," "Hark the Herald Angels Sing."

At first blush I'm equally surprised to find that the editors included "We Three Kings," calling it "one of the most successful modern [carol] examples." (The lyrics and music were written by an Episcopal deacon in New York City a few years before the Civil War.) It's *not* what I'd call a hilarious dance tune. And yet as I give it a second look, I see that it is a musical, even lyrical, drama for the masses—a simple folksy retelling and explication of the gospel story.

It works so well that Sunday school teachers are still able to cajole boys into donning old bathrobes, sobering up (banishing the parodies from their lips if not their minds: We three kings of Orient are / Smoking on a rubber cigar . . .), and shuffling down church aisles, singing the verse-1 trio. "We three . . . bearing gifts."

Occasionally a brave soul (or three) will sing one of the subsequent solo verses in a fashion reminiscent of the Christmas show at Radio City Music Hall: each king presenting a particular gift to the Christ child and explaining its symbolic meaning—which itself weaves the grand story of Christ's purpose and life.

For such a king as this, sings a wise man traditionally called Melchior, I give gold

> *to crown him again—*
> *King for ever, ceasing never,*
> *Over us all to reign.*

And young Gaspar offers frankincense, fit for burning in the presence of God, its fragrance wafting to the heavens:

> *Incense owns a Deity nigh:*
> *Prayer and praising, all men raising,*
> *Worship him, God most high.*

And then an aging Balthazar delivers a grave message as he holds out his gift, a valuable burial salve:

> *Myrrh is mine; its bitter perfume*
> *Breathes a life of gathering gloom;*

> Sorrowing, sighing, bleeding, dying,
> Sealed in the stone-cold tomb.

Three gifts, traditionally seen as symbols of three roles of Christ. In case someone misses the point, Hopkins succinctly brings it all together in the carol's last joyous verse. Nothing subtle here: "Glorious now, behold him arise, / King, and God, and sacrifice!"

Matthew's gospel account of the magi's story makes it clear that their gifts were sincere, direct expressions of worship. And since at least the early third century, Isaiah 60—a description of foreigners bringing treasures accompanied by praise—has been associated with the wise men (vv. 3,6).

> Nations will come to your light,
>   and kings to the brightness of your dawn. . . .
> All from Sheba will come,
>   bearing gold and incense
>   and proclaiming the praise of the LORD.

Three gifts, so appropriate that their story—like the very star of wonder that led the kings to Bethlehem—still guides us to the Light of lights.

Wouldn't it be great if our gifts—to our God, to our loved ones, to strangers—retained that vital spark, carrying a message that speaks across time? Treasures that will be cherished for years to come.

❧

Lord, when I hear the wise men's story, remind me of the significance of their gifts—which we can now see as symbols that remind us of who the Christ child was. As I give to others, help me to choose gifts that will speak beyond the moment.

Part III

Psalms in Songs

The Church with psalms must shout,
No door can keep them out;
But above all, the heart
Must bear the longest part.

George Herbert

Joy to the World

Isaac Watts, 1674 - 1748

Joy to the world, the Lord is come!
Let earth receive her King;
Let every heart prepare him room,
And heaven and nature sing.

As a child Isaac Watts—always a peculiar character—thought and spoke in rhyme. One day this penchant so annoyed his father that he lashed out and whipped the boy—who cried: "O father, do some pity take, and I will no more verses make."

But the resolution didn't hold, nor did his father's displeasure. When he was fifteen, Isaac suffered through yet another in a lifelong succession of dull Sunday-morning church services. His father's sermon wasn't the problem. It was the psalm singing, which droned on; the sacred Scriptures may have been inspired, but the monotonous renditions weren't.

That afternoon over dinner he complained to his father about the hopeless state of contemporary church music. As he later expressed it, "The singing of God's praise is the part of worship nighest heaven, and its performance among us is the worst on earth."

The older Watts listened to his son and posed a challenge: "Give us something better, young man."

The teen went to work. That very evening the Southampton (England) congregation sang a new song penned by young Watts:

> *Behold the glories of the Lamb*
> *Amidst his Father's throne;*
> *Prepare new honors for his name,*
> *And songs before unknown.*

English-language church music would never again be the same. In the next twenty years, Watts, known as the father of English hymnody, would revolutionize the way Christians expressed their praise—with meter and memorable rhyme.

Many of Watts' songs "ran with" the theme of a psalm, where appropriate adding in references to New Testament redemption. To Watts, "Joy to the World," published in 1719, was not a Christmas carol but a loosely paraphrased Old Testament doxology found in Psalm 98. "Joy to the World" picks up in the middle of the psalm (vv. 4, 8–9):

> *Shout for joy to the LORD, all the earth,*
>   *burst into jubilant song with music; . . .*
> *Let the rivers clap their hands,*
>   *let the mountains sing together for joy;*
> *let them sing before the LORD,*
>   *for he comes to judge the earth.*
> *He will judge the world in righteousness*
>   *and the peoples with equity.*

As I reflect on Psalm 98 and this hymn in light of Dr. Watts' story, I wonder why he didn't start with a paraphrase of the psalm's opening line: "O sing a new song." After all, "new song" defines the whole body of Watts's life work. He spent a lifetime repackaging the church's dreary music without harming content, he wrote a "new song" that would transform the praise of his and many subsequent generations. He might even have borrowed the same-metered lines from his very first song, written as a teen: "Prepare new honors for his name, / And songs before unknown."

But no, he skipped the emphasis on the "new" and focused on the joy.

And it seems to have made all the difference.

Watts's exuberant version of Psalm 98 shows signs of immortality, the carol recognized even by millions who see the church as being a relic left over from another time.

> *Joy to the world, the Savior reigns!*
> *Let men their songs employ;*
> *While fields and floods, rocks, hills, and plains*
> *Repeat the sounding joy.*

As he matured, maybe Watts learned an important lesson: old or new, it doesn't really matter. Without joy, the praises are dead. With joy, the music speaks.

❦

Lord, prepare my heart to sing a joyful song. New, or old as the mountains themselves, what does it matter? Just let the praises flow— here, there, everywhere, far as the curse is found.

He Hideth My Soul

Fanny Crosby, 1820 - 1915

He hideth my soul in the cleft of the rock
That shadows a dry, thirsty land;
He hideth my life in the depths of his love,
And covers me there with his hand.

A year out of college, Martha had married the man of her dreams. Four years later her marriage had turned into a nightmare of fear, anger, distrust, abuse. Like a disciplining father, her husband saw it as his role to set her straight, if necessary by force and fist. As for her two toddlers—she lived in fear of how he mistreated them in her absence.

Each week she allowed herself only one night away from home—to take a graduate course at a nearby university. She was away exactly four hours. A one-hour drive into the city, a two-hour class, then the drive home. No after-class conversation or dawdling. No library stop. Just in and out—to get back home to hover over her children. To stand in the gap if anything blew up.

"That drive was the only solitude I had all week," she says, "the only time I was alone—and quiet." Her one chance to hide. "My mind often turned to prayer—and song, usually one particular hymn that was, well, not my style." Martha explains: The tune brought back memories of Sunday-night-church, waltz-time, Hammond-organ music.

And yet years later, the song she naturally disliked seemed Spirit-planted in her mind. She couldn't discount it, and the words upheld and enfolded her as she walked in a parched desert place.

This song, written by Fanny Crosby, is based on images found in Psalm 31:

> *Turn your ear to me,*
> *come quickly to my rescue;*
> *be my rock of refuge,*
> *a strong fortress to save me. . . .*
> *In the shelter of your presence you hide them (vv. 2, 20).*

Crosby herself knew hardship. Blind from infancy, she made a name for herself as a gospel songwriter. And this in the nineteenth century, when physical handicaps were culturally more formidable than now.

A shadow lingers over Fanny's own domestic life. Her only child died as an infant, a loss she would *never* discuss. And though never divorced, in later life she and her husband— whom she always spoke of with affection—lived separately for years. Why? No one knows.

But both Fanny and Martha clung to the assurance that their Lord held them secure and shaded in a rock fortress. But lest that sound impersonal—or the rocks be radiating heat like an old bread oven—the image also included a fleshy component: The Lord "covers me there with his hand."

That rock-sure but personal relationship gave Martha the strength to reach out of her isolation and seek help for herself and her children.

That relationship can uphold you in your crisis. Remember, what the psalmist refers to as a "strong fortress," a few verses later he calls "the shelter of [God's] presence."

A spiritual phrases it yet another way, describing Jesus as a "Rock in a weary land."

A shelter whatever your need.

Lord, allow me to experience you as a Rock of refuge. But
don't let me forget that that protecting shelter is your very presence, the
covering of your hand.

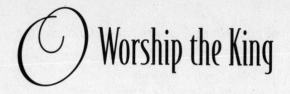

O Worship the King

Sir Robert Grant, 1779 – 1838

O worship the King, all glorious above,
O gratefully sing his power and his love;
Our Shield and Defender, the Ancient of Days,
Pavilioned in splendor and girded with praise.

Last winter on a rainy weekday I wheeled my cart out of the Safeway. It was 5:00 P.M., not my usual time to shop or be at this busy plaza intersection, and I wasn't expecting a forceful, sensual reminder of the God who owns the air we breathe. As if it ruled the dusk, the carillon of some nearby church broadcast the melody of "O worship the King, all glorious above, / O gratefully sing his power and his love."
Knowing the words, I smiled and joined the praises.

Thy bountiful care what tongue can recite?
It breathes in the air, it shines in the light;
It streams from the hills, it descends to the plain,
And sweetly distills in the dew and the rain.

Robert Grant's hymn—based on themes and images of Psalm 104—describes a Creator God who, though not nature itself, is intricately connected to and obviously evident through the created world. Martin Luther described Psalm 104 as "a praise of God from the book of Nature." God is great; you can see it in his ancient but enduring creative work. God, says the psalmist,

> *wraps himself in light as with a garment;*
>   *he stretches out the heavens like a tent. . . .*
> *He makes the clouds his chariot*
>   *and rides on the wings of the wind.*

The psalm is long, thirty-five verses, and with a few digressions follows the Genesis progression of creation: God is the Lord of the light; his fountains water the flora; the animals, the sea creatures—including the mysterious leviathan—all look to God for sustenance and breath. This is a mighty God, worthy of praise.

> *O tell of his might, O sing of his grace,*
> *Whose robe is the light, whose canopy space;*
> *His chariots of wrath the deep thunder-clouds form,*
> *And dark is his path on the wings of the storm.*

That afternoon as I walked through the Safeway parking lot, in the wake of a storm, the witness of Grant's airborne music was particularly powerful because it took me by surprise. To me the song feels so Protestant, so Anglo (written by a member of the British parliament eventually knighted), so "establishment" (in several old hymnals it is printed as hymn number 1, as if it were the mother of all songs). Considering its British, regal aura, its distilling presence felt disconcertingly uncharacteristic of my community. I do not live in a white, Anglo neighborhood. Within a mile of my home you'll find Vietnamese, Korean, and Spanish-speaking churches. Within two miles there's a traditional black Baptist congregation, the Ethiopian Coptics, and, over near the Safeway, a Muslim mosque. This is not to say that most of my neighbors gather for worship. They don't.

That afternoon the carillon's music descended on shoppers and commuters who didn't recognize the song; they didn't

smile at the first ascending notes and eagerly join in with praises
to the "Ancient of Days." And yet at any moment of any day
God invites them—and you and me again and again—to look
to the heavens and the earth, the light and night, the rain and
dew, the created world, and catch a glimpse of the wonder of
the work of God's hand.

> The earth with its store of wonders untold,
> Almighty, thy power hath founded of old;
> Hath stablished it fast by a changeless decree,
> And round it hath cast, like a mantle, the sea.
>
> O measureless Might, ineffable Love,
> While angels delight to hymn thee above,
> Thy humbler creation, though feeble their lays,
> With true adoration shall sing to thy praise.[†]

Lord, open my eyes—and my neighbors'—to see you in your
creation. Prompt me to worship you for your creation, but remind me
that you are the Eternal Being beyond creation who set it all in
motion.

[†]These Grant verses are generally missing from modern hymnals. The last
verse, "O measureless Might," is reminiscent of Psalm 103: God knows we are
dust; angels and all God's works—praise him.

In Heavenly Love Abiding

Anna Waring, 1823 – 1910

In heavenly love abiding,
No change my heart shall fear;
And safe is such confiding,
For nothing changes here.

*A*fter its first verse of generic comfort, this soft hymn is a refreshing take on themes found in Psalm 23: "The Lord is my shepherd." Introducing his book titled *The Shepherd Psalm,* F. B. Meyer asks his reader to "Sing again the old song [psalm] of how all wants are swallowed up in the shepherd love of God." That is also the evident intent of author Anna Waring:

Wherever he may guide me,
No want shall turn me back;
My Shepherd is beside me,
And nothing can I lack. . . .

Green pastures are before me,
Which yet I have not seen;
Bright skies will soon be o'er me,
Where the dark clouds have been. . . .

Waring wrote this hymn when young. Though many of her verbs are in the present tense, the overall tone of the verse carries you into the future: "No change my heart shall fear"; "Bright skies will soon be o'er me"; and the very last line, "And he will walk with me." Her psalm is one of hope, grounded in faith; how can a woman not yet thirty who would live nearly ninety years have any clear comprehension of what pastures, green or otherwise, lie out ahead of her?

What did life have in store for Waring? We don't know many details. She never married. She took her faith seriously; she learned Hebrew so she could get to the heart of the Old Testament, especially the poetry of the psalms. But "good works" didn't take a backseat; an active supporter of the Discharged Prisoners' Aid Society, she visited prisons in Bristol, England, and helped get ex-prisoners on their feet. From what we do know, there's every indication that she held the comfort of the psalm—and the surely good and merciful Shepherd—with her all the days of her life.

As beautiful and reassuring as Waring's hymn is, David's original psalm speaks with more surety. It seems less tentative.

Meyer gives a plausible reason: that the psalm was written not by David the young but by David the aged.

> There is a strength, a maturity, a depth, which are not wholly compatible with tender youth, and seem rather to betoken the touch of the man who has learned good by knowing evil, and who . . . has fully tested the shepherd graces of the Lord of whom he sings. . . .
>
> David the king did not forget David the shepherd boy. . . . The mature experience of his manhood blends with the vivid memory of a boyhood spent among the sheep.

David's song is powerful because it bespeaks the confidence of experience.

And yet there's a wonder in it all—that the psalm's heart-felt message touches the frisky young—hoping for a future—as deeply as it touches the old, ready to rest forever in the house of the Lord. Meyer calls it "the psalm of childhood and of age." What other Scripture passage is read at infant baptisms and at grandfathers' funerals?

Whether you prefer David's original take or Anna Waring's more tentative, hopeful version—or any number of other paraphrases—I encourage you to "sing again the old song of how all wants are swallowed up in the shepherd love of God."

Stand on its promises or praise God for its time-tested truth.

Lord, give me the grace to allow you to be my shepherd. Today. Tomorrow. And forever.

Let All the World in Every Corner Sing

George Herbert, 1593 – 1633

Let all the world in every corner sing,
My God and King!
The heavens are not too high,
His praise may thither fly;
The earth is not too low,
His praises there may grow.

Rev. George Herbert lived in a day when no one expected much from an Anglican clergyman. Many younger sons of prominent families—like Herbert himself—procured pastorates and drew church salaries but left the work of pastoring to underling curates.

"Holy Mr. Herbert," as he was called, had a different, hands-on view of his vocation. In the small town of Bemerton, he preached and prayed, visited the sick and dying; using his own funds, he renovated the dilapidated church and rectory. In fewer than five years as pastor (he died of consumption at age thirty-nine), he gained the love and respect of his entire village, saint and sinner alike.

One Herbert story reveals his character. Twice a week, he walked to the nearby cathedral town of Salisbury where he met informally with several musicians who formed a sort of music club. One day his friends were taken aback to see him arrive very "soiled and discomposed." It seems he had stopped to help a man whose horse had fallen in the mud. The friends chastised him for getting ruffled up. *Shouldn't a man of his stature have walked by on the other side?*

> Herbert replied that the thought of what he had done would be music to him at midnight—and that the omission of it would have made discord in his conscience. "I am bound to practise what I pray for . . . and I praise God for this occasion. Come, let's tune our instruments!"[1]

At these music sessions the repertoire was considerably wider than any allowed in formal worship. Herbert died a generation before Isaac Watts was born. That means the Church of England sanctioned only one form of congregational singing: the Book of Psalms. "The theological beliefs derived from John Calvin . . . united all Protestants in this practice: only God's own Word was worthy to be used in praising Him." But, notes Albert Edward Bailey, Parliament "could not prevent a poet from writing [hymns of 'human composure'] or from singing in his own home, or in social gatherings."[2] And Parliament did not prevent pastor-musician-poet Herbert from writing this poem as a song.

The refrain and first verse of "Let All the World" are reminiscent of psalm phrases. "Sing to the LORD, all the earth" (96:1); "If I go up to the heavens, you are there; / if I make my bed in the depths, you are there" (139:8).

And the second verse is a subtle commentary on the real issues of corporate or private praise in Herbert's—or any—day.

> *The Church with psalms must shout,*
> *No door can keep them out;*

> *But above all, the heart*
> *Must bear the longest part.*

The psalms, though foundationally important to worship, take a second place to the praises of the heart. Of course, the heartfelt praises might *be* the biblical psalms. But then maybe not, testifies Herbert—whose good works were themselves an act of praise, and who left behind a legacy of devotional poetry (of "human composure") still considered among the finest written in English.

Herbert's hymn encourages us to sing the Hebrew psalms. That challenge is one our churches have accepted; much of our contemporary praise music is clearly King David's song packaged for a new generation. But Herbert also challenges us to write a song of our own—to lift up our hearts in spontaneous praise. Words sung at home in the morning. Written in journals. Shared in social gatherings. Songs lived out in beyond-the-call-of-duty, loving deeds—which the Spirit whispers back to us at midnight.

Lord, as I sing your psalms, implant in my heart a fresh, new song. Let me raise my voice with all the world, singing the praises of my God and King.

O God Our Help in Ages Past

Isaac Watts, 1674 – 1748

O God our help in ages past,
Our hope for years to come,
Our shelter from the stormy blast,
And our eternal home.

As a young man Isaac Watts set out to loosely paraphrase the psalms. He had two goals in mind: to make them easy to sing and to interject bits of New Testament revelation. This project culminated in the 1719 publication of a hymnbook containing songs based on all 150 psalms: *The Psalms of David Imitated in the Language of the New Testament.*

Considered Watts's best piece of work, "O God Our Help"—originally "Our God Our Help"—is patterned after Psalm 90: "LORD, THOU hast been our dwellingplace in all generations" (v. 1, KJV). Scholars think a psalmist wrote the confident verses in the midst of a great political upheaval—upon the death of Israel's youthful "good King Josiah."

Several millennia later Watts wrote:

A thousand ages in thy sight
Are like an evening gone:
Short as the watch that ends the night
Before the rising sun.

And in many ways little had changed. In England Watts's generation faced a national crisis of its own. The generous Protestant "good Queen Anne" was near death. None of her six children had survived childhood. Who would take the throne?

Prospects that the crown would go to the queen's Catholic brother panicked the Protestant church, especially Calvinists such as Watts, convinced that they would be harshly persecuted. The throne actually went to Anne's cousin, George, Elector of Hanover (a district in Germany under England's rule). At least George was a Protestant, but even he provided discomfort. King George I was "a foreigner." Born and raised on the Continent, he knew no English. (Even as king he never learned the language.) He was clueless when it came to national customs. And besides, he had a reputation for being uncouth.

In response to this political uncertainty, Watts introduced an updated, even contemporary, Psalm 90. One pointed verse is rarely printed in American hymnals:

> *Under the shadow of thy throne*
> *Thy saints have dwelt secure;*
> *Sufficient is thine arm alone,*
> *And our defense is sure.*

Widely distributed in leaflet form, the hymn calmed a country's fears: One's confidence is in the eternal God—constant from generation to generation—not in earthly rulers whose benevolence or indifference or cruelty will be short-lived in the context of human history.

> *Time, like an ever-rolling stream,*
> *Bears all its sons away;*
> *They fly, forgotten, as a dream*
> *Dies at the opening day.*

Author and friend Fay Angus remembers singing the hymn to observe another transition of power, the end of World

War II. In 1989 Fay traveled to London to join a gathering of
fellow survivors—British and Americans formerly held by the
Japanese as prisoners of war in China.

The commemoration climaxed in a special "service of
thanksgiving" held in Windsor Castle, in the queen's chapel
that holds the burial vaults of five British kings. That day more
than four hundred worshipers praised the good God whose
benevolent reign has endured generation upon generation, as
kings and queens, dictators and presidents have rallied but ultimately been swept away by the rolling stream of time.

I propose that we introduce Watts's hymn-prayer into our
devotional or church calendar, to be sung on election day and
inauguration day—whether we fear or anticipate what a new
administration might bring upon us. We have a King who rules
in a realm beyond politics. And he shall reign forever and ever.

*Lord, when we feel uncertain about a new political administration
or policy, remind us that you are the everlasting God whose reign outlasts
the men and women who are given authority over nations. Remind us
that your rule is good and just. That you are our help and hope.*

$\mathcal{H}$e Took My Feet from the Miry Clay

African-American Spiritual

He took my feet from the miry clay.
   Yes, he did.
And placed them on the rock to stay.
   Yes, he did.

$\mathcal{L}$ike a good hymnbook of any era, the Book of Psalms includes songs of praise that seem to be written and sung in a realm above the daily grind. They are about who God is. "Great is the LORD, and most worthy of praise" (48:1); "The LORD reigns, let the nations tremble" (99:1).

But it also contains a good many more subjective songs about "me"—what I (the song's writer or reader) need or want or have received from God.

Consider Psalm 40:1–3, attributed to King David. It's a short-short story, with beginning, middle, and end. I paraphrase: *I needed to be rescued. I called on God and waited. God delivered me, by pulling me out of "the miry clay" and setting my feet upon a rock. My desperation lifted; I sang a new song—of praise. Many people will see what God has done for me; they will hear my song and trust God.*

The story, including the strong image—sinking in quicksand contrasted with standing on a solid slab of marble—

has held its ground, having been revisited in the American tradition.

There's the old spiritual version. "What the Negroes sang
were the psalm tunes of the whites. . . . What finally emerged as
the spiritual was the expression of a people torn violently from
one tradition and thrust against their will into another."[3] I can
imagine this psalm being sung responsively across rows of
tobacco.

> *He took my feet from the miry clay.*
> > *Yes, he did.*
> *And placed them on the rock to stay.*
> > *Yes, he did.*
>
> *I can tell the world about this:*
> *I can tell the nations I'm blessed,*
> *Tell them that Jesus made me whole,*
> *And he brought joy, joy to my soul.*

And there's also the white nineteenth-century camp
meeting version, called "He Brought Me Out." Henry L.
Gilmour, a dentist who spent his summers directing camp
choirs, tacked this psalm-based refrain onto gospel lyrics by
Rev. H. J. Zelley, for which Gilmour was composing a tune:

> *He brought me out of the miry clay,*
> *He set my feet on the Rock to stay;*
> *He puts a song in my soul today,*
> *A song of praise, hallelujah!*

Zelley's four stanzas fill in the Psalm 40 story line, and his
last verse hammers out the psalmist's evangelistic challenge:

> *I'll sing of his wonderful mercy to me,*
> *I'll praise him till all men his goodness shall see;*
> *I'll sing of salvation at home and abroad,*
> *Till many shall hear the truth and trust in God.*

Neither of the American songs short-circuits the ancient story; both acknowledge God's grace.

God moved my feet from the quicksand to the rock.

Yes, he did.

And then the songs spread the good news. And so can we.

I can tell the world about this.

Yes, I will.

Lord, I thank you for your goodness to me—your having "brought me out." And forgive me for not taking the opportunity to spread the good news of your deliverance with others. Give me an opportunity today.

Part IV

Lines Learned as Children

Let those refuse to sing
Who never knew our God,
But children of the heavenly King
May speak their joys abroad.

Isaac Watts

esus Loves Me

Anna Warner, 1820 - 1915

Jesus loves me! this I know,
For the Bible tells me so;
Little ones to him belong;
They are weak, but he is strong.

This simple children's song has its high-minded critics who call it schmaltz. Bless them. May they someday learn . . .

This same song has been memorialized by an eminent scholar whose name would hold ground on a shortlist of twentieth-century theologians. One day the aging Karl Barth was asked a "deep" question. Would he—could he—summarize the essence of his theological discoveries?

Barth had a ready response: "Jesus loves me! this I know. For the Bible tells me so." The first couplet of a children's song crisply condensed his lifelong journey in faith.

The song itself was first published a century before Barth's citation, and even then the words were written as a response—to a dying boy's request of his Sunday school teacher: "Sing." Not that this was a flesh-and-blood death. The sickly Johnny was a character in a popular but now long-forgotten novel, titled *Say and Seal,* coauthored by Anna Warner and her sister Susan. In this fictional world the impromptu lullaby "Jesus Loves Me" calmed the feverish child and introduced the reader to the assuring words now sung around the globe by children of all ages.

It takes a child's heart to appreciate this song, just as it takes a child's heart to know the heart of our loving God. Jesus made it clear: "Anyone who will not receive the kingdom of God like a little child will never enter it" (Mark 10:15).

My friend Elsie recently spent a warm summer afternoon as a volunteer visitor in a hospital long-term-care unit. Intent on delivering inspiration to one particular woman, she dressed in a bright dress, bought a handful of flowers, and wore a smile. These visual signs of cheer did not dispel the gloom in the patient's room. "Nothing could be said to cheer her up," Elsie remembers. Until . . . "I began to sing softly, 'Jesus loves me! this I know, . . . Little ones to him belong. . . . Yes, Jesus loves me!'"

And a second verse—not part of Warner's original lineup: "Jesus loves me! He will stay / Close beside me all the way. . . .'"

Elsie continues: "When I started, she became very quiet. And with the last note, she could focus on hope. We talked of God's wonderful love for each of us and the hope of eternal life. After a short prayer, it was evident that peace had filled her heart."

In their book *Songs for Renewal,* Janet Janzen and Richard Foster tell of a man dying after a long battle with cancer. Knowing his hour was at hand, he started singing Warner's lullaby "and praying for God to receive his spirit."

> *Jesus loves me! He who died*
> *Heaven's gate to open wide;*
> *He will wash away my sin,*
> *Let his little child come in.*

Janzen continues, "In the early hours of the morning he was indeed welcomed into the arms of Jesus."[1] Like a child. Like the children of another age, as described by the evangelist: "And [Jesus] took the children in his arms, put his hands on them and blessed them" (Mark 10:16).

In the words of another sentimental song: "Jesus loves the little children." All the children. Young and old. Healthy or feeble. He loves you. Are you child enough to claim it?

❧

Lord, I want to know your love for me—not just on an intellectual level. Allow me to feel—emotionally—the assurance of your love. That means I have to become a child at heart? I'm not sure I know what that means, but . . . work your love in me.

Jesus Bids Us Shine

Susan Warner, 1819 – 85

Jesus bids us shine
With a clear, pure light,
Like a little candle
Burning in the night.

This one is beyond me: I've heard of a church that has banned the singing of this song—not because the children wouldn't know what the word *bid* means but because the lyrics patronize children. Who can figure? Have they similarly cut "This Little Light of Mine"? Maybe they should expurgate the bidding Sermon on the Mount: "You are the light of the world. . . . [People do not] light a lamp and put it under a bowl. Instead they put it on its stand, and it gives light to everyone in the house. In the same way, let your light shine before men" (Matthew 5:14–16).

The song, meant for children, was written by Susan Warner, an immensely popular—though now forgotten—writer of adult and young adult novels, many with biblical settings. Before the Civil War her novel *The Wide, Wide World* (published under the pseudonym Elizabeth Wetherell) hit the fiction "best-seller lists"—number two, behind *Uncle Tom's Cabin*. Susan often collaborated with her sister Anna, who received less literary recognition but remains the remembered; *Bartlett's Familiar Quotations* reduces the familial legacy to Anna's best-loved line: "Jesus loves me! this I know, / For the Bible tells me so."

The sisters Warner, never married, lived and worked together in their stately homestead, called Good Crag, on Constitution Island in the Hudson River. And from their corner, they let their lights shine—like a lighthouse—back to the mainland. They took their writer's life—a solitary profession— seriously, but they didn't exactly squirrel themselves away from society. For years they chose to accept a mission—on Sundays sending a boat to nearby West Point to pick up cadets from the military academy; they welcomed the young men—grown boys—at their hearth for a Bible study followed by tea and dessert.

And for this they were well-loved. Sister Susan died thirty years before Anna who lived to be ninety-five. Both women were highly honored in their burial at West Point.

I say good for them. There's nothing wrong with accolades (far too often they come only posthumously). But Jesus' "You are the light of the world" sermon says that human acclaim should not be our number-one motivation for service or generosity . . . for accepting a goodwill mission or embarking on a ministry. When Jesus bid his followers to let their candles shine—not under a basket but out in the open air—he laid out a clear reason: so that as people see your good works, they will "praise" not you but "your Father in heaven" (Matthew 5:16).

From your corner of the world—whether it's a Hudson island or a city high-rise or a suburban acre—let your light shine. For Jesus' sake, accept your mission. And then give yourself permission to sing a lilting censured song:

> *In this world of darkness;*
> *So we must shine,*
> *You in your small corner,*
> *And I in mine.*

Lord, Light of the world, let your light shine out from within me as I choose to accept the mission—the good works—you have prepared for me. May you receive the glory. Now and forever.

Onward, Christian Soldiers

Sabine Baring-Gould, 1834 – 1924

Onward, Christian soldiers,
*   Marching as to war,*
With the cross of Jesus
*   Going on before.*

Catholics have a centuries-old tradition—teaching their children that they are Christian soldiers. Commissioned to defend the faith. To stand firm in the face of opposition. To join the long procession of kingdom witnesses marching behind the cross, under the banner of Christ.

As a fourth-grader, Beth was sobered by the church's challenge—and by her older sister's exaggerated warning of Beth's upcoming confirmation service: "The bishop smacks you. Don't worry about it, but you've got to be ready."

Actually, says Beth, the bishop simply laid a light hand on her cheek—a symbol of a formerly formidable slap, itself a symbolic reminder of the opposition a believer could expect. As a sobered soldier, says Beth, "I knew I had a job to do; I had to uphold the faith."

Though Beth is no longer a Catholic, the bishop's underlying message stuck. Beth's significant hymn—to this day? "Onward, Christian Soldiers."

Militaristic metaphors of the church are out of fashion. And in this day of political polarity, one might be wise to use the biblical army images with discretion, lest we be justifiably accused of reckless sniping and pillage.

And yet as a church—as believers—we do have enemies to wage war against; using spiritual armor and gear that "are not the weapons of the world" (2 Corinthians 10:4), we are to fight "not against flesh and blood, but against . . . the spiritual forces of evil" (Ephesians 6:12).

And we do well to teach and show our children that the Christian faith is full of paradox. Yes, we are sheep safely grazing under the watchful eye of the Good Shepherd. At the same time we are called to choose whom we will serve; we are called to bear witness to our allegiance to the King of Kings.

I think Sabine Baring-Gould, an Anglican pastor serving his first year at his first church—the small wool-mill town of Horbury Bridge, Yorkshire—must have understood the mysteries. For his parish children he wrote the assuring, lulling "Now the Day Is Over" *and* the rousing "Onward, Christian Soldiers." (See the following devotional entry, "Now the Day Is Over.")

Baring-Gould, a prolific writer, left us his own account of the origins of his marching processional, originally sung—in May 1864—not to "our" tune but to the then-familiar theme of the slow movement of Haydn's *Symphony in D*.

> One Whitmonday it was arranged that our school should join its forces with that of a neighboring village. I wanted the children to sing when marching from one village to the other, but couldn't think of anything quite suitable, so I sat up at night resolved to write something myself. "Onward, Christian Soldiers" was the result. It was written in great haste. Certainly nothing has surprised me more than its popularity.

Whitmonday? Translation please? Let's start with Whitsun, a Britishism for Pentecost; as a concession to the cold weather, in northern England, Easter baptisms were postponed fifty days until "White Sunday," so called because of the white robes worn by the new converts. The holiday lasted through Monday (Whitmonday or Whitmon).

And in Yorkshire, the holy day was the occasion for an annual "procession of witness": Children paraded the streets. Following a leader lifting high a cross. Carrying banners that made their allegiance evident to the wider community.

> *Christ, the royal Master,*
> *Leads against the foe;*
> *Forward into battle,*
> *See his banners go!*

Several stanzas of Baring-Gould's warhorse are forgettable, but his finale stands still as an invitation to all—young or old—to accept the commission, to spread the Good News, to join the procession of kingdom witnesses. Maybe marching, fighting, sobered here and now. For a season. But surely not for long. Come along. Fall in. Forward, march.

> *Onward then ye people,*
> *Join our happy throng;*
> *Blend with ours your voices*
> *In the triumph song;*
> *"Glory, laud, and honor*
> *Unto Christ the King!"*
> *This through countless ages*
> *Men and angels sing. . . .*
>
> *With the cross of Jesus*
> *Going on before.*

❧

*L*ord, show me what it means to be a soldier of Christ—following the cross, the symbol of your kingdom, and carrying your banner as a witness of my allegiance to you.

Now the Day Is Over

Sabine Baring-Gould, 1834 – 1924

Now the day is over,
Night is drawing nigh,
Shadows of the evening
Steal across the sky.

My six siblings and I would agree; we are haunted by evening prayers that in times past spoke to us of endings, losses, departures.

There were the deadly lines of our first memorized prayer: "Now I lay me down to sleep, I pray the Lord my soul to keep; If I should die before I wake, I pray the Lord my soul to take."

Then there were the strangely comforting vesper hymns our father loved to lead. Late Sunday afternoons our parson pa would choose the congregational songs for the evening service. Often, probably not as often as I now imagine, he turned to the section of shadowy selections: "Day Is Dying in the West"; "Abide with Me! Fast Falls the Eventide"; "Sun of My Soul"; "Now the Day Is Over."

My father—an imposing pacesetter—led these night songs as if they were somber dirges. Maybe he'd read Homer, who called sleep "the brother of death." Or Shakespeare: "sleep, death's counterfeit."

Maybe that wasn't it at all. Maybe he was a boy again, hearing or singing soft, slow lullabies.

> *Through the long night-watches*
> *May thine angels spread*
> *Their white wings above me,*
> *Watching round my bed.*

Maybe he was a padre praying a night's comfort on his children—those sleeping under his roof and others beyond his reach.

> *Grant to little children*
> *Visions bright of thee;*
> *Guard the sailors tossing*
> *On the deep blue sea.*

A hundred years earlier another pastor, the young Anglican Sabine Baring-Gould, wrote "Now the Day Is Over" for the children of his first parish—children who worked in woolen mills by day and studied at Baring-Gould's one-room school by night. (See the devotional on "Onward Christian Soldiers," also by Baring-Gould.) I can imagine the vesper prayer, "Now the day is over . . ." as the pastor's nightly blessing over his flock. A community's lullaby.

> *Jesus, give the weary*
> *Calm and sweet repose;*
> *With thy tenderest blessing*
> *May our eyelids close.*

As a child I didn't see it, but I now note that Baring-Gould's song stands apart from many evening hymns in that he had the good sense to welcome the new day even as he bid the old good-bye. He did not allude to death, and he eventually wound his way to tomorrow and its holy hope.

> *When the morning wakens,*
> *Then may I arise*

Pure and fresh and sinless
In thy holy eyes.

Buried here is an ancient mind-set that we who are no longer children might do well to revive. Consider the Genesis account of creation, where a "day" starts at dusk. "There was evening, and there was morning—the first day," and the second and third. The Jewish day has always commenced at sundown—a visibly evident ending marking also a very good beginning.

Eugene Peterson notes:

> [This] Hebrew evening/morning sequence conditions us to the rhythms of grace. We go to sleep, and God begins his work. . . . Always grace is previous and primary. We wake into a world we didn't make, into a salvation we didn't earn.
>
> Evening: God begins, without our help, his creative day. Morning: God calls us to enjoy and share and develop the work he initiated.[2]

In recent years I've tried to see the hours of rest as preparation more than as recovery, as a bond to life, not a bridge to death. Grace for a new day begins when the daylight ends.

I don't know why my father *always* sang his favorite night music in funereal fashion. Maybe it was simply a providential plot—for haunting a houseful of children with evening hymns. And here I proffer my own—for a new generation of children:

Now the day is over.
Now a new begins.
God's grace rests upon us.
Come, let's nestle in.

There Is a Green Hill Far Away

Cecil Frances Alexander, 1818 – 95

There is a green hill far away,
Without a city wall,
Where the dear Lord was crucified,
Who died to save us all.

We mortals will always be surprised at what remains of our lives or of our centuries. This is evident in the pages of our songbooks. Any number of songs originally written for children have wound their way into hearts now old and hymnals edited for and read by adults. A prime example is Cecil Frances Humphreys Alexander's much-loved "There Is a Green Hill Far Away." Before his death, William Alexander, eminent Anglican archbishop of Ireland, had a wry grip on the realities of the twists and turns of history. He who presided over the church's rules and rites said he would ultimately be remembered only for being the husband of the woman who wrote "There Is a Green Hill Far Away." Right he was.

Author of more than four hundred hymns, Mrs. Alexander, as she was known, generally wrote for young Sunday school children, in an attempt to bring the Christian faith and feasts down to their level.

"There Is a Green Hill" came to her as she sat at the bedside of a critically ill girl, who lived to relate the incident; as a child she was not called to test the gate-locks of heaven.

> *He died that we might be forgiven,*
> *He died to make us good,*
> *That we might go at last to heaven,*
> *Saved by his precious blood.*
>
> *There was no other good enough*
> *To pay the price of sin;*
> *He only could unlock the gate*
> *Of heaven, and let us in.*

When published in a collection of Alexander's *Hymns for Little Children,* "There Is a Green Hill" stood among several (including her memorable "Once in Royal David's City" and "All Things Bright and Beautiful") that explicated specific lines of the Apostles' Creed.

Alexander lived in Londonderry, a city bound by a stone wall and surrounded by rolling hills. Having never seen Jerusalem, she is said to have fancied a particular nearby knoll to be "like Calvary." In this regard, she may have been inventing her own version of history.

In subsequent verses she clearly lays out the basics of the historically orthodox understanding of the Creed's "I believe": *in Jesus Christ who "suffered under Pontius Pilate, was crucified, died, and was buried."* For your redemption and mine.

On this count was she writing fact or fiction? She does have her critics. Is there a "price of sin"—or a penalty of sin and price of redemption? Is her whole notion of atonement "outworn"? Do scholars hunting for the historical Jesus prove the Christ of our creed a merely mythical figure? Do they put the poems of Alexander on a shelf, never to be dusted off?

I'm no theologian, but I find insight in the comments of philosopher C. Stephen Evans. After giving an overview of gospel-discrediting Jesus scholarship, he affirms that many

scholars conversant with ancient languages and texts see
the historical evidence as consistent with historic Christian faith.

However, it is equally vital to realize that Christ's
church does not stand or fall with the changing fashions
of a contemporary academic field. My Christian beliefs are
not primarily grounded in historical scholarship but in the
testimony of Christ's church and the work of Christ's
Spirit, as they witness to the truth of God's revelation.[3]

In the preface to *The Course of Empire,* Pulitzer-prize-
winner and historian Bernard De Voto noted that although
"history abhors determinism," it "cannot tolerate chance."[4] And
it is by no chance that our faith—in the redemptive death of
Christ—has survived the millennia since his resurrection.

"I believe," says the church of Christ.

And all the people said, "Amen."

*Lord, this song gives me such a simple rendition of the Good
News of your redemption. Give me a new understanding of what it
means, as I bear witness to the Word and as I live under the grace it
offers me. Lord, I believe. Help my unbelief.*

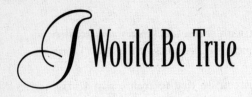

I Would Be True

Howard Arnold Walter, 1883 – 1918

I would be true, for there are those who trust me;
I would be pure, for there are those who care;
I would be strong, for there is much to suffer;
I would be brave, for there is much to dare.

If you want to get somewhere in life, you need to write a personal mission statement. Or is it a vision statement? Or is it a short list of life goals (as opposed to objectives)?

The life-is-to-be-managed lingo confuses me. There must be a simpler way—maybe that modeled by young Howard Arnold Walter. A recent graduate of Princeton, Walter sailed to Japan for a year—to teach English at Waseda University. From Tokyo he mailed his Connecticut mother a two-stanza poem written as a private exercise. "My Creed" listed eight idealistic "I woulds."

Impressed with the son she had raised, Mother Walter submitted the verse to *Harper's Bazaar*. An editor said yes, and the magazine published the personal creed in 1907. Cecilia Margaret Rudin astutely comments that the poem "combines true social and ethical action with a certain boyish and gallant spirit of chivalric ideals."[5]

Walter returned to the States, went to seminary, and then, ready to change the world, he sailed to India as a YMCA staff member—and there, still a young man, he died of influenza in 1918.

In 1911 Walter's creed inspired a tune, composed by Joseph Peek, and the song quickly spurred a generation looking for courage. Including a nine-year-old schoolboy.

"It was the Pittsburgh of 1925," writes my friend and mentor, Dr. Kenneth L. Wilson, "when the steel mills owned the sky and the air. While my mother spent a year in a sanitarium, I lived with an aunt and uncle."

Ken transferred into a new school, where he felt outclassed by the mysteries of long division. "It was as if I had been dropped into another country that was speaking another language." It was a hard, lonely year that is somewhat redeemed in Ken's memory by having learned one song in religious, "released-time" classes at the Methodist church.

The heartening words were distributed to the students: the first verse (see above) and the second:

I would be friend of all, the foe, the friendless;
I would be giving, and forget the gift;
I would be humble, for I know my weakness;
I would look up, and laugh, and love, and lift.

Ken survived the year and returned home—to his mother's welcoming arms. He left that chilly school, with two treasures: the code to unlock the "divided-bys" and a creed that has shaped his life. "The words meant enough even then to cause me to remember them all this time."

Now reflecting on his four-score years—a life of honor, a career as a leading religious journalist defending truth, befriending the needy around the world—Ken soberly wonders: for a young boy did the words mean what they mean now "for one who has lived out most of a long life and who knows how far short of the shining 'would-bes' life sometimes comes"?

Age may have dampened his "boyish and gallant spirit," and yet Ken still sings the song, a creed that, says Rudin, "contains almost all that we need in life."

Well, almost. It seems that a slightly more mature Howard Walter identified an element missing from his original purposeful statement. Some time before his premature death, he tagged on a third verse:

> *I would be prayerful through each busy moment;*
> *I would be constantly in touch with God;*
> *I would be tuned to hear his slightest whisper;*
> *I would have faith to keep the path Christ trod.*

"I Would Be True"—the total package. A life mission statement? Maybe not as the life managers would define it.

But as a guide for life, it was good enough for my friend Ken. As a young boy. As a magazine editor and husband and father. As an older man with time still left for the new day's "I woulds," reality-tempered as they may be.

And it's good enough for me.

How about you?

❧

Lord, help me to be true to you and to the ideals to which you point us, not because my salvation hinges on my ability to measure up. But because my witness may direct someone else to you and the redemption you offer.

Tell Me the Stories of Jesus

William Henry Parker, 1845 – 1929

Tell me the stories of Jesus
I love to hear. . . .
Scenes by the wayside,
Tales of the sea,
Stories of Jesus,
Tell them to me.

In the summer of 1885 a warmhearted Baptist businessman in Nottingham, England, settled in for a Lord's Day rest. His mind settled on the young students in his Sunday school class. Wanting attention. Needing direction. Always tugging at him with one request: "Tell us another story."

Before the day was over, William Parker had written the lyrics of this song made memorable by the soothing melody it later inspired, when a publisher ran a contest to find a fitting tune.

As I peruse my cache of hymnbooks I am reminded of similar first lines, none written expressly for children: Fanny Crosby's "Tell me the story of Jesus / Write on my heart every word" was published a few years before Parker penned his lines—an ocean away.

Parker and Crosby probably knew the then-popular "Tell Me the Old, Old Story," written twenty years earlier by Britisher Kate Hankey. Her "Tell Me" is drawn from a long poem titled "The Story Wanted," in which the narrator begs a gospel story: "Tell me the story slowly ... often ... softly ... always ... simply, / As to a little child."

Tell me—tell the children—the story. Many Christians have grasped hold of the challenge. Others are rediscovering their heritage. I recently read of a mainline pastor who reshuffled leadership priorities—when he discovered his Sunday school children could not name one Bible story that had any relevance to life here and now. Suddenly retelling stories to children seemed more important than tending to endless administrative tasks.

"Tell me the story." It's a request of every generation of children. Every year at her birthday dinner, my young friend Glenna asks her mother the same question: "Tell me the story about the day I was born."

And I vividly remember one summer evening in 1985, just a hundred years after William Parker wrote "Tell Me the Stories of Jesus." I was visiting my parents for a weekend, and another guest graced the house: my youngest niece, a toddler still in diapers, just beginning to string words into sentences. With granddaughter Elizabeth snuggled at his side, my father "read" through Peter Spier's *Noah's Ark* picture book. Telling the story. Naming the animals. Walking the rainbow. Closing the book.

And then came Elizabeth's supplication, as basic as it can be: "Read again."

Repeat the stories. Our children need to hear them.

Long ago and far away does matter. Here and now.

First let me hear how the children
Stood round his knee;

And I shall fancy his blessing
Resting on me.

Lord, give me a new appreciation of the old, old story that you chose to leave with us. Your story. Our story. The Good-News story. Give me opportunity to tell the story in a fresh way to someone—of any age—who is eager to hear it.

Part V

Lessons from the Gospels

And when in scenes of glory,
I sing the new, new song,
'Twill be the old, old story
That I have loved so long.

Kate Hankey

In the Garden

C. Austin Miles, 1868 - 1946

I come to the garden alone,
While the dew is still on the roses;
And the voice I hear, falling on my ear,
The Son of God discloses.

Austin Miles used the word *vision* to describe the encounter that led to his writing "In the Garden." The setting was Philadelphia, where Miles was employed as an editor for a music publisher. March 1912. At home Miles sat in a windowless room of his own—a combination study, photo lab, and music parlor. He reached for his Bible. "It opened at my favorite chapter, John 20," he later explained.

"It opened." One wonders at the passive construction. Was the binding bent because he so frequently turned to this passage? Was the Spirit turning the pages?

John 20. What's the story? John's account of the Resurrection: two angels and then a "gardener" ask a distraught Mary Magdalene why she is crying. Because "they"—or is it "you"?—have taken my Lord away.

And then gardener Jesus says one word that transforms the scene: "Mary."

He speaks her name, and she knows who he is. Rabboni.

As Miles read the familiar story, he felt as if he were a bystander on-site. In another century, as if this were an episode of the old Walter Cronkite television series: "You Are There: At the Garden Tomb."

"Under the inspiration of this vision," Miles explained, he wrote "In the Garden," the words coming to mind as quickly as he could write them down. (And the text stands as first written, never being revised.) Later in the day Miles wrote the music.

Miles described his activity as "reading" John 20; some would say he was praying. Scripture reading as prayer? It's an ancient art lost on many Christians intent on *studying* the Scripture. One prayer pattern involves imagining oneself in a gospel scene. "You Are There." Ignatius of Loyola advised believers to "see the [gospel] persons in [your] imagination, contemplating and meditating in detail the circumstances surrounding them, and [you] will then draw some spiritual profit from this scene." He goes on, suggesting that we imagine the sounds, smells, tastes, and touch "always endeavoring to draw some spiritual fruit from this" application of the senses.

In his classic *Lord, Teach Us to Pray,* Alexander Whyte says, "You open your New Testament. . . . And, by your imagination, that moment you are one of Christ's disciples on the spot. . . . At another time, you are Mary Magdalene"—in the garden recognizing the voice of her Lord as he speaks her name.

Though Austin Miles described himself as an observer in the story, he wrote "In the Garden" in first person, as if he had stepped into Mary's shoes: Jesus is walking and talking directly with him—and you and me. Calling us by name.

> *And he walks with me, and he talks with me,*
> *And he tells me I am his own,*
> *And the joy we share as we tarry there,*
> *None other has ever known.*

Consider placing yourself in the garden scene described in John 20. Read and meditate. Don't expect an experience of visionary proportions; don't expect to be given a song that captivates a country. Expect personal, spiritual fruit. Give God permission to speak to your heart through your imagination.

Lord, you physically walked this earth for just a few years, but you graciously left us an account of your life and ministry. As I read the Gospels, allow me to see Christ relating to me; allow me to respond with an open heart. I also pray that you would guard my imagination. Keep me centered on the truth of your Word.

Pass Me Not, O Gentle Savior

Fanny Crosby, 1820 - 1915

Pass me not, O gentle Savior,
Hear my humble cry;
While on others thou art calling
Do not pass me by.

A Hebrew notion of hell: a state of being alone, forgotten, blotted from memory—passed on, passed over, passed by.

It's a child's cry—*Don't leave me. Don't forget me. Don't abandon me here alone*—stretched out over eternity.

"Pass Me Not," one of the most popular evangelistic hymns of the Dwight Moody era, was Fanny Crosby's visceral response to a sinner's cry—her heart pierced with the providential prayer of one abandoned man living an earthly hell.

And now for the rest of the story:

William Doane, a wealthy entrepreneur, and Fanny Crosby eventually teamed up to make emotive if not beautiful music together—collaborating on more than a thousand songs. Their initial meeting—Doane having tracked Crosby down on a visit to New York City—led to the writing of "Pass Me Not."

Acquainted with Crosby by her poetic reputation and a brief correspondence, Doane was surprised at what he found on the lower west side of Manhattan: a diminutive middle-aged blind woman living in a dilapidated tenement. Crosby welcomed Doane into her attic apartment. He returned a few days later; Crosby accepted a challenge he placed before her: Could she—would she—write a poem titled "Pass Me Not, O Gentle Savior"?

Crosby typically wrote lyrics for a specific melody or as the muses struck; Doane's request—to "run with" a prescribed but tuneless first line—went without inspiration for several weeks until . . .

Crosby walked into a room full of men whom society had cast aside. Criminals locked away in a fortress. Crosby, speaking at evangelistic services in a prison near her home, overheard one prisoner's desperate prayer: "Good Lord! Do not pass me by!" Do not turn your back on me. Do not ignore me, forget me, neglect me.

Crosby went home that night and penned four verses and a chorus. Doane subsequently wrote the tune appropriate to the sinner's memorable supplication.

> *Savior, Savior,*
> > *Hear my humble cry;*
> *While on others thou art calling,*
> > *Do not pass me by.*

I see the promise of the prayer's answer in the Bible's first story: Adam and Eve fallen from favor, knowing their nakedness, not yet knowing to plead the Lord's mercy. They heard God passing by, "walking in the garden in the cool of the day," and for fear and for shame "they hid from the LORD God among the trees" (Genesis 3:8).

From that time to this, foolish sinners have futilely hid from God—and there under the bushes they have dug themselves a hellhole.

From that time to this, God has called out with one consistent question: "Sinner, where are you?"

What's traditionally called the sinner's prayer ("Lord, have mercy on me a sinner") comes from another biblical passage, this time more clearly redemptive. Luke 18 tells of a blind beggar who hears that "Jesus of Nazareth is passing by." With that news the castaway calls out, "Jesus, son of David, have mercy on me!" Do not ignore me, forget me, neglect me. Heal me. Restore me.

And here's the end of the story. Jesus says to us, "Whoever comes to me I will never drive away. . . . everyone who looks to the Son and believes in him shall have eternal life" (John 6:37, 40).

Come out from hiding. Humbly ask to be accepted, and he will not pass you by. He asks the first question: *Sinner, where are you?* He makes the first claim: *You may have left me. But I haven't left you.*

Lord, sometimes I think you have forgotten me, neglected me, dejected me, passed me by. Remind me that you are the one who is always asking, "Sinner, where are you?"

Be Still, My Soul

Katharina von Schlegel, b. 1697
trans. by Jane Borthwick, 1813 – 97

Be still, my soul; the Lord is on thy side;
Bear patiently the cross of grief or pain. . . .

This is not a song meant for "it's-great-to-be-alive" mornings. Even the tune with which it's come to be associated *(Finlandia* by Sibelius) seems somber. Paradise is lost. Trouble is brewing. Maybe disaster has already struck.

Taken by itself, the line "Be still, my soul" is a self-addressed command; pop psychology calls it "self-speak," and it can be very effective. I have smiled to hear a toddler muttering to himself, repeating what he'd heard from his mother, convincing himself that her advice was trustworthy: *Don't be afraid. Don't be afraid. Don't be afraid.* The mantra mattered.

But there is more to this hymn than psychobabble. There is a justified reason for keeping one's head if one's faith reaches beyond the trouble so as to embrace the Lord of the universe.

Be still, my soul: the waves and winds still know
His voice who ruled them while he dwelt below.

Think in terms of the night described in Mark 4:37–41. Jesus and the disciples were in a small boat, crossing the lake:

A furious squall came up.... The disciples woke [Jesus] and said to him, "Teacher, don't you care if we drown?"

He got up, rebuked the wind and said to the waves, "Quiet! Be still!" Then the wind died down and it was completely calm.

He said to his disciples, "Why are you so afraid? Do you still have no faith?"

They were terrified and asked each other, "Who is this? Even the wind and the waves obey him!"

Be still. Jesus said it first to the wind and water. But then, more subtly, he said it also to his colleagues. "Why are you so afraid?" *Don't you know you can and should calm down. Because I am here. Be still.*

Ruth Luckey of Houghton, New York, tells of the day some fifty years ago when this hymn's message cut through her sorrow:

On August 5, 1944, word came that my fiancé had been killed in the crash of a P–51 fighter plane in England. I immediately rode twenty miles to be with his parents. The next day, a Sunday morning, I sat alone at the end of a pew in the big Methodist Church in Westfield, New York; his parents did not feel up to attending. His older sister was playing the organ. I remember nothing of the service—except the closing hymn, which spoke to my hurting heart as I sang. (I *did* sing.) "Be still, my soul; the Lord is on thy side. / Bear patiently the cross of grief and pain. / Leave to thy God to order and provide.... Be still, my soul."

This hymn, originally written in German by a woman who may have been a Lutheran nun, repeats the title phrase,

"Be still, my soul," six times in three verses. But those same lines refer to God—the reason for one's composure—at least eight times. Because of God, be still.

Phillips Brooks, author of "O Little Town of Bethlehem," has suggested that it is often easier to find a stillness of soul when one is outdoors.

> The sweet and solemn influence which comes to you out [from] the noontide or the midnight sky does not take away your pain, but it takes out of it its bitter- ness. It lifts it to a higher peace. It says, "Be still and wait." It gives the reason power and leave and time to work. It gathers the partial into the embrace of the universal.

This quote does not refer directly to God. By itself this might be psychobabble. But Phillips is the same man who wrote: "Many of us who call ourselves theists are like the [peo- ple] who, in the desire to honor the wonderful sundial which had been given them, built a roof over it. Break down the roof; let God in on your life."

That's the message of von Schlegel's hymn: "Let God in on Your Life." And in so doing know that you can and should be still. Even on a morning when paradise is way out of reach.

Lord, help me to look to you to take the bitterness out of any pain I face.

At the Cross

Isaac Watts, 1674 – 1748
refrain by Ralph Hudson

At the cross, at the cross where I first saw the light,
And the burden of my heart rolled away,
It was there by faith I received my sight,
And now I am happy all the day!

A few years out of college, I was angry with the world, and God had been silent so long I was sure he was angry with me. Early one Sunday evening I paced my apartment until the walls closed in. Then I walked briskly around the block, once, twice.

On the third time around I saw a middle-aged black man climbing the steps of a small red-brick church about which I knew nothing except what was evident from the sign: The Fire Baptized Holiness Church.

Wearing patched jeans and flip-flops, I asked the man if I would be welcome. "Anyone can come to church," he answered. And I walked through the sanctuary door, flanked by white-gloved women passing out paper fans printed with Martin Luther King profiles.

As I slipped into a back row, a young girl dressed in starch pointed at me. "She can't stay here; she's got pants on."

The shushing mother smiled at me. "Of course she can."
I was welcome, albeit a curiosity.

As was the service to me. It started with fifteen minutes
of fervent prayer around the altar. I stayed in my seat, contemplating the words painted on the wall—"I am the way, the
truth, and the life"—and silently praying my anger: "But *where*
are you, God?"

Then singing—"Everything's all right, in my Father's
house." Over and over and over. A dance of blessing. Up and
down the aisles. Jumping till the pews shook.

And testimonies, most confessing unfaithfulness yet
thanking God for his faithfulness.

More songs—and with no hymnbooks (no hymn racks!),
overheads, or handouts. Everyone knew all the verses.

"Leaning, leaning on the everlasting arms." I sang along
and kept praying. *God, come to me as you have come to them.*
Nothing happened. *See it doesn't work for me,* I finally shrugged.

But then God broke through—with the old, out-of-
fashion words of Isaac Watts, sung in slow, deliberate, half-time:

Alas, and did my Savior bleed?
And did my Sovereign die?
Would he devote that sacred head
For such a worm as I?

And the refrain, not by Britisher Watts, but by American
evangelist Ralph Hudson: "At the cross, at the cross where I
first saw the light, / And the burden of my heart rolled away."
At that word, my burden of anger lifted as I anticipated the
next lines, sung by the Fire Baptized: "It was there by faith I
received my sight, / And now I am happy all the day!"

We blessed singers went on and on—repeating verses and
refrains. Where was God? "The way, the truth, and the life" was
not only painted on the wall, he was not only "a worm" nailed
on a cross (see Psalm 22), he was with me and within me, and

eager to let his presence be known as I humbled myself at his bleeding feet.

God doesn't restrict his blessing to those who dance down the church aisles. If you're burdened with anger or feeling God's absence, try meeting him at the cross. Loosen your pack and let him rip it off.

"Come to me, all you who are weary and burdened, and I will give you rest. . . . For my yoke is easy and my burden is light" (Matthew 11:28, 30).

Lord, at the foot of your cross I drop my burden of anger—just drop it. Release it. Let me walk away with a new yoke that is easy to wear, light with grace.

Was a Wandering Sheep

Horatius Bonar, 1808 - 89

I was a wandering sheep,
I did not love the fold,
I did not love my Shepherd's voice,
I would not be controlled.

ℛev. Horatius Bonar had a deep concern for men, women, and children who were lost—wandering outside the fold of the Good Shepherd. He also had a keen imagination and a "way with words" that he put to good use. An admirer of Bonar's hymns said that under Bonar's sway "the massive theology of the Reformation . . . breaks into deep and tender melody, a crystal river from the rock."

Bonar first wrote songs for Sunday school children, making the Scripture stories and ideals accessible to young souls. He printed the songs on handbills for kids to take home. Eventually he branched out to hymns for adults.

He wrote songs, some six hundred in all, spontaneously in notebooks when traveling on trains; some he scribbled on scraps of paper with caricature doodles in the margins. He published many—one per issue—as editor of the *Quarterly Journal of Prophecy,* and they caught on, helping to mold a new denomination: The Free Church, independent from the government-controlled Established Church of Scotland.

The childishly simple "I Was a Wandering Sheep" is not Bonar's most memorable (that claim might be made of "I Heard the Voice of Jesus Say," written for children, or "Here, O My Lord, I See Thee Face to Face," a Communion hymn), but I want to think that Bonar's heavenly reward will be grand for having penned this one song, which God has used to soften and summon hardened hearts, young and not-so.

In his classic *One Hundred and One Hymn Stories* Carl Price relates the conversion story of a scoffing, skeptical teenager; as her first confession of faith, she dramatically recited Bonar's poem. The sheep's story was her own, even the last verse: "No more a wayward child, I seek no more to roam. . . ."

And I was deeply moved when I read how the Spirit used Bonar's hymn to "get through" to Tom Enneking, a middle-aged career criminal.

At age thirteen, Tom says, "I just decided that I was going to get into a life of crime." A ten-year prison term—for first-degree murder—didn't deter him from his path of destruction. Paroled in 1972, Tom was in and out of prison until 1985, when, drunk in a California jail cell, Tom was roused by a sobering thought: *I'm forty-two years old, and I'm still where I was at fifteen.*

That wake-up call was followed by another. Several nights later the jail intercom blared an announcement for Catholic Mass. Tom, raised an Episcopalian, had never taken religion seriously. "But all of a sudden, I wanted to go to Mass," says Tom.

When officers said all worshipers would be strip-searched, Tom had second thoughts. *I'm not as spry as I used to be. I don't want to strip in front of all these guys. I'm going back to my cell.* "But as I said that, I started unbuttoning my shirt. I was thinking, *What are you doing, man?* Today I believe I was under the power of the Holy Spirit."

Once in the pew, Tom read a song in the hymn-book.[1]

Yes, it was Bonar's "I was a wandering sheep ... I would not be controlled ... I loved afar to roam."

The Shepherd sought his sheep ...
He followed me o'er vale and hill,
O'er deserts waste and wild;
He found me nigh to death,
Famished and faint and lone;
He bound me with the bands of love,
He saved the wandering one.
The words struck to the heart.

And then in the chapel service the priest noted that angels rejoice when one lost sinner—one lost sheep—comes to the Father. Tom remembers, "All I could think about was that *I* could make *God* happy."

That evening Tom was welcomed into the Shepherd's fold, and he has chosen to start a new life and stay "close in." Released from prison in 1989, Tom is an active believer living out his faith as a volunteer countywide coordinator for Angel Tree, a Christian ministry to prisoners' children.

Here on earth Tom is still singing Bonar's last verse: "I love my tender Shepherd's voice, / I love the peaceful fold."

"Across the other side," Rev. Bonar is, I trust, still rejoicing with the Shepherd who leads the celebration over the return of every one: "Rejoice with me," said Jesus at the end of the Parable of the Lost Sheep (Luke 15:6). Rejoice because the lost has been found. "I tell you, there is rejoicing in the presence of the angels of God over one sinner who repents" (Luke 15:10).

And again I say rejoice. Celebrate your own salvation. Stop and name person after person you know who once was lost but now is found. Celebrate their salvation. Celebrate doubly if God chose to work through your witness or words, as he used Horatius Bonar to draw Tom Enneking off the craggy cliff and into the fold.

Lord, my Shepherd, you have blessed me with the assurance of my own salvation. Never let me take that lightly. Allow me to use that security to reach out to others who are wandering. And then celebrate when the lost return to your fold.

The Day of Resurrection

John of Damascus, c. 675 – 749
trans. by John Mason Neale, 1818 – 66

The day of resurrection!
Earth tell it out abroad;
The Passover of gladness,
The Passover of God. . . .

Our hearts be pure from evil,
That we may see aright
The Lord in rays eternal
Of resurrection light.

Eastern worship cares not about the clock."[2] And that is particularly evident at Easter, the most festive day of the year: the day of resurrection!

The ancient Orthodox Easter liturgy owes much to John of Damascus—an eighth-century theologian, philosopher, preacher, and, some claim, the Greek church's greatest poet.

John—born in Damascus to a family well-connected in Muslim circles—lived in a monastic community just outside Jerusalem. From his holy mountain he studied, preached, and wrote, his masterpiece being eight odes—the Golden Canon for Easter Sunday—of which "The Day of Resurrection!" is the first.

In 1862 John Neale published a loose translation of the hymn in his *Hymns of the Eastern Church*. Along with the text he printed a lengthy description of a nineteenth-century Orthodox Resurrection service. Last week I attended a Greek Easter vigil, and I quickly sensed that little had changed in 150 years. Much of the service was not in English, so for me the worship was primarily a visual experience. The most obvious symbolism plays tomblike darkness against the break-in of resurrection light.

The celebration starts at midnight (after nearly an hour of preparatory choir-chanted canons—on the order of biblical ballads). The church is dark, even the votive candles extinguished. One lone candle remains lit at the altar and in expectation everyone in the church holds a long white candle.

And then—Christ bursts his prison. Christ is risen. Christ is risen.

From the priest's taper, acolytes light candles in the front pews. And then the flame spreads quickly, each person turning to ignite the wick of the person behind. Front to back, the Easter light sweeps the full house. Raising the candles above their heads, the congregation repeatedly sings (in Greek) the ancient-but-suddenly-new story: "Christ has risen from the dead, / by death trampling upon death / and has bestowed life / to those in the tombs."

The liturgy continues for several hours, the lit candles tightly gripped all the way to the last lines—written by another early father, John Chrysostom: "Christ is risen, and the tomb is emptied of the dead; for Christ, having risen from the dead, is become the firstfruits of those who have fallen asleep. To him be glory and power forever and ever. Amen."

In the service here is what impressed me most: the white candles were never blown out. Men and women carried the light of Christ with them out of the church, out into the night, out into the family car. I watched minivans pulling onto the road—rolling slowly home toward suburban driveways—and inside the candles still flickered. Was I imagining the sight? No. And the priest offered an explanation. Back home the candles would burn all night; the resurrection light would kindle the fire of an oil lamp that burns all year.

As translated by Neale, John of Damascus opened the Golden Canon for Easter by announcing that Christ had brought us over "from death to life eternal," from tomblike darkness to breakout brilliance.

And the Orthodox service itself reminds believers that the resurrection light is to be "carried out" beyond the sanctuary of believers into the world, beyond the dawn of resurrection. You might say the light of Christ "cares not about the clock." It shines through all the days and nights of the calendar year. In and through your life and mine.

Because the Lord is risen. The dark grave is open.

Indeed.

❧

Lord, because you have risen from the dead, every morning can be Easter to me, every day a day of resurrection. This day I lift a candle to your resurrection light and ask that you give me opportunity to share that light with others living in darkness.

Wake, Awake, for Night Is Flying

Philip Nicolai, 1556 – 1608
trans. by Catherine Winkworth

Wake, awake, for night is flying:
The watchmen on the heights are crying,
Awake, Jerusalem, arise!
Midnight's solemn hour is tolling,
His chariot wheels are nearer rolling,
He comes; prepare, ye virgins wise.

Seminary hadn't prepared Rev. Philip Nicolai to deal with this pestilence: thirty burials a day. Thirty parishioners in Unna, Westphalia (Germany), dead from the bubonic plague. His Lutheran parsonage overlooked the church cemetery, once topped with grass and wildflowers but now gashed like a plowed field and bulging with bodies, thirteen hundred within six months.

One death in particular had hit him hard: fifteen-year-old Wilhelm, whom he tutored in theology. Why was such a promising life cut short? There was no telling. And for all he knew, Nicolai himself could be the next to go down.

Well, he was ready to meet his Maker.

As a testimony to that fact, Nicolai wrote a book of meditations, titled *A Mirror of Joy,* which included several hymns, one being "Wake, Awake" (or "Sleepers, Awake"). He said he wrote *A Mirror of Joy*—and chose that title—"to leave behind me (if God should call me from this world) as the token of my peaceful, joyful, Christian departure, or (if God should spare me in health) to comfort other sufferers whom he should also visit with the pestilence."

Nicolai survived, living ten more years, spanning the new century.

And his hymn lives on, repeatedly translated and updated for new generations. To this day the song is sung primarily in Advent, a season liturgically focused on Christ's second coming. The song is based on an Old Testament wake-up warning (Isaiah 52:1, 8),

> *Awake, awake, O Zion,*
> > *clothe yourself with strength.*
> *Put on your garments of splendor. . . .*
> *Listen! Your watchmen lift up their voices . . .*
> *When the LORD returns to Zion,*
> > *they will see it with their own eyes.*

and an "end-times" gospel parable; Nicolai gave the hymn an unwieldy descriptive title: "Of the voice at midnight and the wise virgins who meet their heavenly bridegroom"—clearly referring to Matthew 25:1–13, Jesus' story of ten bridesmaids. Remember the characters and the action? Five young women are ready and wise. Five are foolish and unprepared, out of oil and left in the dark at midnight, when the bridegroom who has been "a long time in coming" is finally announced: he's coming. It's time for the wedding procession. Beware. Some, who are not ready, will be turned away from the feast.

Nicolai chose to challenge the faithful with a parable often used to condemn the damnable. He didn't dwell on the group that was shut out; his troupe was ready for the call. Whenever it may come—at midnight, at 4:00 A.M., at dawn— they will quickly light their lamps and

> *Rise up, with willing feet*
> *Go forth, the Bridegroom meet:*
> *Bear through the night your well-trimmed light,*
> *Speed forth to join the marriage rite.*

This was, after all, published in a book meant to mirror joy and comfort, a book written for the faithful waiting for their final redemption, which is somewhere, near or far, on the other side of this present pestilence.

We, especially when young, expect the end "tomorrow"— if ever—not today. It would be so much easier if we knew when we would be "called" by death or the last trump. It would be easier if the Bridegroom would return on schedule, like daylight saving time in April. If we knew exactly when, we would not be caught off guard.

But Nicholai echoed Jesus: *You may well be surprised at the timing of the Bridegroom's coming, but you don't need to be found wanting or unprepared.* Jesus told the story of ten bridesmaids waiting for a wedding feast to begin. Five were ready and wel- comed into the celebration. It might have been ten, if all had been wise, if all had kept watch, oil replenished, lamps burning, ready to greet the host.

We *can* be ready to go with joy.

Lord, give me strength to keep watch when I'm suffering hard- ship. Give me the desire to keep watch when I'd rather be amused by the trivial pursuits of this world.

Part VI

Words That Challenge

I was singing when the Lord told me. . . .
Shirley Ann Caesar

Stand Up, Stand Up for Jesus

George Duffield, Jr., 1818 - 88

Stand up, stand up for Jesus,
Ye soldiers of the cross;
Lift high his royal banner,
It must not suffer loss.
From victory unto victory
His army shall he lead,
Till every foe is vanquished,
And Christ is Lord indeed.

In 1858, three years before the outbreak of the Civil War, revival swept the city of Philadelphia. People responded particularly to the hard-hitting messages of Dudley Tyng, a young, vivacious, abolitionist Episcopal priest.

In March at a noontime, weekday YMCA gathering of five thousand men, Tyng let it rip, basing his sermon on Exodus 10:11: "Go now ye that are men, and serve the LORD" (KJV). As he spoke, he acknowledged that his radical call for repentance was potentially offensive. He hoped his audience would not take umbrage at his challenge, but, he continued, "I would rather that this right arm were amputated at the trunk, than that I should come short of my duty to you in delivering God's message."

That afternoon more than a thousand men enlisted in the Lord's army. And Tyng returned home newly challenged to lead the charge, lift high the banner. Little did he know the impending twists of fate.

A week later, studying in his home office, Tyng took a break. He walked out to the barnyard to encourage a mule—whose circular plodding fueled a corn-shelling machine. Alas. Patting the mule, Tyng caught his billowy sleeve in the wheel cogs. Tyng lost his arm. And within days his life.

At his son's deathbed, Tyng's father asked if he had a message for his colleagues. Tyng's last words proved to be his most memorable: "Tell my brethren of the ministry, wherever you meet them, to stand up for Jesus."

That message, relayed at Tyng's funeral, gripped a friend, Rev. George Duffield. The next Sunday at Philadelphia's Temple Presbyterian Church, Duffield preached on Ephesians 6:14, a Pauline challenge couched in military language: "Stand firm," wearing the whole armor of God. Duffield ended his sermon with a poem he had penned that week: "Stand Up, Stand Up for Jesus . . ." (Am I perverse to wonder if there is hidden meaning in the lines: "The arm of flesh will fail you, / Ye dare not trust your own"?)

A parishioner printed the poem in leaflet form. It was picked up by a magazine and within a few years sung heartily around Union army campfires.

And still is sung today.

Last Sunday morning our church organist played its familiar tune. The congregation joined in. A stooped, old man sitting behind me sang lustily. And as the last chord died out, he whispered loudly, spontaneously, as if he'd forgotten he was in church: "That was a good one!"

I smiled. Was he a veteran of a great war? I expect so. After church he slipped out the door before I could ask. The song struck something in his spirit. A call to take courage and stand for his Lord—even as his years and life slipped from him.

A musician tells me this song is a favorite at nursing homes, especially among men and women confined to wheelchairs—people who can't physically stand. What does the song mean to someone whose options are limited?

In search of an answer I went scrounging for a haunting article I'd clipped some years ago. Richard Mouw writes: "We are called to be obedient where we are located, with the resources that are available to us, and in the light of our present understanding of God's will."

Mouw continues, relating an eye-opening exchange between him and sociologist Peter Berger. When a younger, harsher Mouw had suggested "that every Christian is called to engage in radical obedience to God's program of justice, righteousness, and peace," Berger had challenged Mouw's grandiose view of obedience.

> Somewhere in a retirement home, [Berger] said, there is a Christian woman whose greatest fear in life is that she will make a fool of herself because she will not be able to control her bladder in the cafeteria line. For this woman, the greatest act of radical obedience to Jesus Christ is to place herself in the hands of a loving God every time she goes off to dinner.[1]

Radical obedience. Standing firm. What does it mean for you?

Stand up, stand up for Jesus!
The trumpet call obey . . .
Ye that are [his] now serve him
Against unnumbered foes;
Let courage rise with danger,
And strength to strength oppose.

Lord, give me courage to stand firm, for your kingdom and for your sake.

He Who Would Valiant Be

John Bunyan, 1628 – 88
adapted by Percy Dearmer, 1867 – 1936

He who would valiant be
'Gainst all disaster,
Let him in constancy
Follow the Master.

*I*f not for the *Prince Valiant* Sunday cartoon strip, the word *valiant* might be classified with the archaic. Until recently enlightened by the dictionary, I would have said it meant "chivalrous"—something no one is anymore. But the word isn't nearly that complicated or outdated. It's a matter of having courage, being brave.

"He Who Would Valiant Be" (sometimes titled "To Be a Pilgrim") is a significantly adapted version of a poem in *The Pilgrim's Progress,* by John Bunyan, until recent years one of the world's most-read books, the grandfather of all English novels.

Bunyan's text of valor was not set to music until early in the twentieth century, when it was substantially altered. William Reynolds notes that Percy Dearmer, editor of the 1906 *English Hymnal,* "removed such words as 'hobgoblins,' 'foul fiends,' 'lion,' and 'giant' lest they shock some worshipers."[2] (There's nothing new about "politically correct" editing.)

Though a fine, noble hymn (admittedly finer in the hands of Bunyan than Dearmer), "To Be a Pilgrim" lacks something when it stands alone, apart from the conversational context of Bunyan's narrative. Let me explain.

Bunyan named his characters by their prominent vice or virtue: Ignorance, Talkative, Mr. Money-love, Hopeful, Mercy, Valiant-for-truth. . . . These men and women populate the allegorical tale of Christian, a pilgrim walking from the City of Destruction to the Celestial City; "part 2" of the story relates the corresponding journey of Christian's wife, Christiana.

Toward the end of her sojourn, Christiana and her travel guide, Great-heart, meet young Valiant-for-truth, who tells of his own pilgrimage. Heeding the message of Mr. Tell-true, Valiant left home and headed for the Celestial City despite dire parental warnings: that he would "go over the Valley of the Shadow of Death, where the hobgoblins are, where the light is darkness, where the way is full of snares, pits, traps. . . ." The potential obstacles—real or imagined—go on for paragraphs.

Great-heart finally asks, "And did none of these things discourage you?"

No.

Why?

Because "I still believed what Mr. Tell-true had said, and that carried me beyond them all," says Valiant.

Great-heart carefully rephrases the explanation: "Then this was your victory, even your faith."

Valiant agrees. Yes, "I believed" and then stepped onto the road and "fought all that set themselves against me, and by believing am come to this place."

With that, Valiant breaks into song:

Who would true valour see,
*   Let him come hither;*
One here will constant be,
*   Come wind, come weather. . . .*

Who so beset him round
    With dismal stories,
Do but themselves confound—
    His strength the more is.
No lion can him fright,
He'll with a giant fight,
But he will have a right
    To be a pilgrim.

Hobgoblin nor foul fiend
    Can daunt his spirit;
He knows he at the end
    Shall life inherit.
Then fancies fly away,
He'll fear not what men say;
He'll labour night and day
    To be a pilgrim.

By itself the hymn makes a strong plea for standing tall, undaunted by foes physical (lions) or spiritual (foul fiends) or imagined (dismal stories). But it does not lay out reasons for Valiant's undergirding, overcoming constancy. *Why* is there "no discouragement [that can] / make him once relent / his first avowed intent to be a pilgrim"?

Valiant is grounded in faith in the truth—faith in the One who is the Way, the Truth, and the Life. (Another Bunyan character named Too-bold is last seen by the side of the road in an unrousable sleep of exhaustion; bravery in and of itself won't sustain us for the long journey.)

We would do well to tie this hymn's theme to the context in which it was first written. As Great-heart said: Valiant Pilgrim, "this was your victory, even your faith." (See 1 John 5:4–5: "This is the victory that has overcome the world, even our faith. Who is it that overcomes the world? Only he who believes that Jesus is the Son of God.")

I think of a nineteenth-century paraphrase by John Yates: "Faith is the victory . . . that overcomes the world"—and lions and hobgoblins, real and imagined.

For valiant pilgrims, faith is the bridge between valor and victory.

❧

Lord, I want to be brave. And I want to know the victory that overcomes the world. Increase my faith in the One who has already overcome any obstacle I face.

Trust and Obey

John Sammis, 1846 – 1919

When we walk with the Lord
In the light of his Word,
What a glory he sheds on our way,
While we do his good will
He abides with us still,
And with all who will trust and obey.

One night in the mid-1880s, when Dwight L. Moody was preaching in Brockton, Massachusetts, his "team" opened the floor, requesting spontaneous testimonies from the audience.

A nervous young man stood and expressed his doubts and then his intentions: "I am not quite sure—but I am going to trust, and I am going to obey."

Hearing such a witness, God wrote that man's name in the Book of Life. Hearing such a genuine faith despite unanswered questions, Moody's musician, Daniel Towner, wrote down the memorable sentence.

Towner mailed the quote and a brief description of its context to his friend Rev. John Sammis, who quickly wrote the four-line refrain to "Trust and Obey." Sammis later added the five verses. He mailed the package back to Towner, who came up with the tune.

"Trust and Obey." For several generations of churchgoers, the words were as familiar as a King James motto. And the phrase has become the life-theme of Bruce Miller, of Corning, New York. Fifteen years ago, just as he and his wife were facing the joys and responsibilities of being middle-aged first-time parents, Bruce developed throat cancer. Doctors got that under control. But then melanoma crept up. Spared again. More recently he has survived heart trouble and bypass surgery. And suffered with a puzzling neurological disease that incapacitated his arms and hands.

The second half of life hasn't been easy, and yet Bruce chooses to trust his present and his future to his Lord. Recently, just as Bruce was gearing up to return to his job after his latest ailment, he told me he chose to view life as an "adventure." He went on to tell the story of one particularly difficult stint in the hospital. A social worker came by every day, asking him a round of questions. She named a succession of "feelings" categories, waiting after each word for him to rate how he felt on a scale of one to ten. *Happy? Depressed? Tense?* Ten meant "couldn't be higher," a realm reserved for the extreme.

"One of the categories was *trust*," Bruce remembers. And after a week or so, the social worker mused aloud as she scanned Bruce's chart: "When we come to *trust*, you always give a ten."

Bruce smiled at her and acknowledged that his trust was not in his doctors or their prescriptions but in the Lord whom he had for years chosen to obey.

> Not a grief nor a loss,
> Not a frown nor a cross,
> But is blest if we trust and obey.
> Trust and obey,
> For there's no other way
> To be happy in Jesus,
> But to trust and obey.

I wonder if evangelist Dwight L. Moody was thinking of "Trust and Obey" when he wrote this summary of the Christian walk: "The blood [of Christ] alone makes us safe. The Word alone makes us sure. Obedience [to God] makes us happy." He seems to be addressing the issues at the heart of the new believer's statement: "I am not quite sure—but I am going to trust, and I am going to obey."

We don't know what became of that young man who inspired a song that still urges believers to trust their Lord and obey his precepts. I choose to believe that after his Brockton experience he saw life as an adventure.

What better way to live—

> *For the favor he shows,*
> *And the joy he bestows,*
> *Are for them who will trust and obey.*

Lord, I'm not always "quite sure," and yet I choose to trust you with my life. As I walk the path of obedience, fill my heart with joy, eagerly expecting your favor and blessing.

The Battle Hymn of the Republic

Julia Ward Howe, 1819 - 1910

Mine eyes have seen the glory
of the coming of the Lord;
He is trampling out the vintage
where the grapes of wrath are stored.

Julia Ward Howe had an eye for spotting injustice, evil, man's inhumanity to man. From Boston she and her husband, Samuel, edited *The Commonwealth,* an abolitionist (Free Soil) paper.

They did more than print words. They helped fugitive slaves. As a young man Dr. Howe, a surgeon, had gone to Greece to help with "war relief"; he was the first director of America's first school for the blind. And Mrs. Howe was the first president of the New England Woman Suffrage Association. They supported Dorothea Dix in her campaign for social reforms on behalf of the mentally ill. Dr. and Mrs. Howe— among the cultural elite of their day—identified a long list of social wrongs in need of righting.

And their God was growing impatient, angry—"on the march"—because good Christian men and women were not.

Julia wrote "Mine Eyes Have Seen the Glory" at the prompting of a pastor friend. In April 1861 Confederate troops had attacked Fort Sumter in South Carolina. Lincoln had mustered federal troops and called for a naval blockade of Southern states. In July Union soldiers had run in retreat out of Manassas, Virginia, just west of Washington. A "rebellion" was beginning to look like war.

In December the Howes, their friend, and the governor of Massachusetts traveled to Washington. On that trip they were invited to visit and review troops camping outside the District. The guests spent the night in a tent, near soldiers sitting at campfires singing the popular "John Brown's Body." It seems the pastor noted that such a good tune deserved more inspiring words. Might Mrs. Howe—an established poet—want to work up something better? That very night—writing in the dark, unable to sleep—she "saw the glory"; the Lord had "loosed the fateful lightning of his terrible swift sword."

In February 1862 the six-verse poem (two verses are virtually never printed) was published in the *Atlantic Monthly,* where an editor titled it "The Battle Hymn of the Republic." A Union chaplain taught the song to troops, and it swept the North like an epidemic.

I marvel at the survival of this highly unusual, graphic song: God trampling grapes of wrath (see Isaiah 63), sifting hearts, marshaling a menacing army; you'd better watch out. It's staying power might be credited to its powerful melody. But you don't hear the Mormon Tabernacle Choir belting out "John Brown's Body." There's something deeper that speaks to singers and hearers who see injustice and want someone—maybe God, maybe their politicians—to do something to stop it. (The injustice, of course, is always caused by some "other"—an enemy with whom God is angry—not by me or mine.)

It's not surprising that this song crept into Martin Luther King's speeches. The historic march from Selma to Montgomery ended with a King speech now titled "Our God Is Marching On!" And his last public words—the conclusion of a sermon delivered the night before he died—were "I'm not fearing any man. Mine eyes have seen the glory of the coming of the Lord."[3]

The end of Howe's hymn—as dramatically sung by choirs at state occasions—grows calm as a holy night:

> *In the beauty of the lilies*
> > *Christ was born across the sea,*
> *With a glory in his bosom*
> > *that transfigures you and me;*

And then you and I—the transformed ones—are challenged by a trick phrasing:

> *As [Christ] died to make men holy;*
> > *let us live to make men free.*

Let it sink in: Howe isn't calling us to make the world holy; that's God's job. She says our work is about freedom and justice. But there's more: though Howe's wartime original read, "Let us die to make men free," editors long ago changed a word; the song as we now sing it doesn't suggest we *die;* it dares us to *live* out the campaign for justice and truth. Doing good. Confronting wrong. Speaking out and standing in for the poor and oppressed. Setting wrongs right. Putting one foot in front of the other.

And I suggest we are able to keep our stride in that freedom march only as we step behind the Lord's blaring trumpet, being fully assured that it "shall never call retreat."

After all, our God is marching on.

Lord, make me sensitive to the injustices I see—the ways my fellow brothers and sisters are held captive by the bureaucracies we create that dehumanize men, women, and children whom you created and for whom you died. Help me to see where I can live to make men and women free. But seeing isn't enough. Give me the desire and grace to act—to live out the commission to act justly and love mercy and walk humbly.

Yield Not to Temptation

Horatio Palmer, 1834 – 1907

Yield not to temptation,
For yielding is sin;
Each victory will help you
Some other to win . . .

Yield Not to Temptation" was written shortly after the Civil War. Horatio Palmer, a professional musician, said the song came to him as "an inspiration." His recollection of the day draws a stark contrast between musical theory and music.

> I was at work on the dry subject of "Theory" when the complete idea flashed upon me, and I laid aside the theoretical work and hurriedly penned both words and music as fast as I could write them. I submitted them to the criticism of a friend afterward, and some changes were made in the third stanza.

In Palmer's explanation ("I laid aside the theoretical work") I see hints of a larger reality: our Christian faith will never "be music" to anyone's ears if we do not get beyond theories—the details of doctrines or traditions. But there's more.

We need to get beyond the momentary "flash" of insight or feeling and test our faith in the real world.

Palmer lived in an era when the church was willing to sing itself a real, not theoretical, challenge. A lot has changed since then, including church music. Tim Stafford noticed this recently, as he perused a section of a sixty-year-old hymnbook. He was startled at "how different these hymns are from any my church sings today. We sing praise songs and hymns, sweet words of love for God, but we have few of these bracing 'sermons in song.'"[4]

Stafford ultimately stings his reader, concluding that we do not sing many bracing sermons because "we are too fat and too comfortable. . . . We do not want to be saints or heroes."

A life of faith involves more than hearing or singing "sweet words of love for God." Maybe we *need* to revive the sentiment of Palmer's musical sermon: "Yield not to temptation."

Brace yourself; Palmer starts his challenge in a commanding tone: *Yield not. Fight onward. Shun the evil. Disdain the bad. Be earnest.* One gets tired thinking about the effort it takes to stay the course and live by biblical restraints: "Don't grumble against each other" (James 5:9); "Put off falsehood" (Ephesians 4:25); "He who has been stealing must steal no longer" (Ephesians 4:28); "Don't show favoritism" (James 2:1). Not to mention the baser prohibitions. The list is long, even if one reads only the New Testament epistles. *Yes, sometimes I'd rather stick to the theory of restraint and not actually practice it.*

Ultimately we all have to make a personal choice. Do we really want to resist temptation? Do we really want to be holy—say nothing of heroic?

For those of us who can answer yes, Palmer provides something more than a terse "buck up." Ultimately Palmer's song is reminiscent of a seventeenth-century exhortation by Fénelon, who said that there are "two things that we can do against temptations. The first is to . . . [avoid] all exposure to temptation." (He further clarifies that not all temptations can be avoided.) Our second defense, he continues, "is to turn our eyes to God in moments of temptation, to throw ourselves immediately upon the protection of heaven, as a child, when in danger, flies to the arms of its parent." And such heavenly help is the overriding theme of Palmer's gospel song refrain:

> *Look ever to Jesus, he will carry you through.*
> *Ask the Savior to help you,*
> *Comfort, strengthen, and keep you;*
> *He is willing to aid you,*
> *He will carry you through.*

The choice is ours. We can live in the world of religious theory, never testing our faith. We can choose to "avoid" tempting situations. We can choose to brace ourselves and "yield not." But the sermon isn't complete without the reassurance that we are not stranded, abandoned in our resistance to the tempter. "God is faithful; he will not let you be tempted beyond what you can bear" (1 Corinthians 10:13).

Maybe being a saint isn't as formidable as we fear.

Lord, give me your strength in the face of temptation.

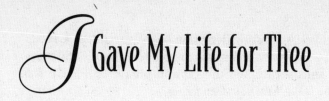

I Gave My Life for Thee

Frances Ridley Havergal, 1836 – 78

I gave my life for thee,
My precious blood I shed,
That thou might ransomed be. . . .
What hast thou given for me?

This song has never been among my favorites.

As a kid learning to play the piano, I pounded the life out of the unimaginative tune—one of the hymnal's easiest, no sharps, no flats, no tricks.

And the words—written as if by Jesus addressing you or me as a disciple—do not draw me to service motivated by *gratitude*. Rather, they drag me down with guilt. I hear a stereotypical martyr mother saying, "After all I've done for you . . . you should be grateful." Duty-bound debt.

And yet I write of this song, viewing it differently in the context of its origin and the author's life.

As a young woman Frances Havergal traveled from her home in England to advance her education in Düsseldorf, Germany. While on the Continent, in a pastor's study, she saw a motto printed beneath a Sternberg painting titled "Ecce Homo." The portrayed scene is Christ at his trial, whipped mercilessly, wearing a crown of thorns and a purple robe meant for mockery. He's standing between a crowd demanding death and Pilate, who says, "Ecce Homo": "Behold the Man."

Sternberg's arresting depiction of Jesus' trial struck Havergal, who paused to contemplate the biblical event. Before leaving the scene, she copied the caption-phrase, translated: *I did this for you. What have you done for me?*

Later, back home in England, she noticed the line in her notebook, recalled her emotional response to the painting, and quickly embellished the caption. She wrote a poem of five stanzas, each ending with a pointed challenge: What have *you* given to . . . left for . . . borne for . . . brought to . . . the Christ?

Pausing to read through her completed verse, Havergal thought poorly of her endeavor, and threw the paper into the fireplace. Yes, into the fire.

But it didn't burn.

Retrieving the lines, she eventually showed them to her father, who suggested they be saved. The next year the poem was printed as a pamphlet, then in a magazine, then with its own tune in an American Sunday school songbook.

Years later she wrote what would become one of her most famous hymns, "Take My Life." The first phrase is reminiscent of the earlier "I Gave My Life," but here she claims the "I-my" as her own: "Take my life and let it be / Consecrated Lord to thee. . . ."

A few lines of a Havergal letter further connect her two songs. The "what have I given for Christ?" question is poignantly answered in the context of these later lines: "Take my silver and my gold, / Not a mite would I withhold." Her letter:

> "Take my silver and my gold" now means shipping off all my ornaments—including a jewel cabinet which is really fit for a countess—to the Church Missionary Society where they will be accepted and disposed of for me. I retain only a brooch for daily wear . . . also a locket. . . . Nearly fifty articles are being packed off. I don't think I need tell you I never packed a box with such pleasure.

This giving-up is no duty-bound debt. It is no casting away of the unsatisfactory endeavor. It is sacrificial—something precious relinquished as Havergal consecrated her life to the God who asks no more of us than he asked of himself.

In her relatively short life (forty-two years), Havergal wrote what has been called a "huge volume" of hymns. Time has borne away the memory of all but a score, including these two: "Take My Life" and the earlier "I Gave My Life"—the poem thrown into the fire.

Intended for destruction—like Christ led by the crowd to Calvary.

But not destroyed—like Christ whose executioners did not have the final say.

At Jesus' trial Pilate said, "Behold the man" (John 19:5 KJV), beaten bloody. With spiritual insight John the Baptist said, "Behold the Lamb of God, which taketh away the sin of the world" (John 1:29 KJV).

> *I gave my life for thee . . .*
> *That thou might ransomed be,*
> *And quickened from the dead.*

This death would result in life—an abundant life that could prompt a young woman to give away what she considered a "jeweler's shop"—with delight.

Two biblical men—Pilate and John the Baptist—saw one Son of God from two radically different perspectives.

And Havergal's story allows me to see new meaning in a throwaway line—Jesus' hypothetical question: "What have you given for me?"

⁓

Lord, open my eyes to show me who you are and what you did for me. Allow me to feel such gratitude that I open my hands and my heart. Generously. Because I want to. Not because I have to.

O for a Thousand Tongues

Charles Wesley, 1707 – 88

O for a thousand tongues to sing
My great Redeemer's praise,
The glories of my God and King,
The triumphs of his grace.

Would you give a workshop at our women's retreat?"
I didn't give a ready response. "Let me pray about it," I said.
When it came to writing, I felt confident. But speaking? The few times I'd formally addressed a group, I'd groped for words. Faltered through sentences. I'd left the disappointed gathering disheartened and eager to get back to my solitary craft.

But, with some trepidation and much faith, I did accept this new invitation. *I'll stretch myself and go for it.*

This time I prepared more thoroughly and this time things "clicked." I spoke with new confidence. I didn't stammer my way through the session; I found words and touched a chord. The women left animated and inspired.

I left exhilarated and also relieved. I could enjoy the rest of the weekend now that my challenge was over.

But was it? I think not.

My presentation is not what I remember most clearly about that weekend retreat ten years ago. The real challenge came during the final Sunday worship service, as we sang a Charles Wesley favorite, "O for a thousand tongues to sing. . . ."

Wesley wrote this exuberant song on the first anniversary of his conversion—a day of celebration.

I knew the words—didn't need a book—even for the fifth verse:

Hear him, ye deaf; his praise, ye dumb,
Your loosened tongues employ;
Ye blind, behold your Savior come;
And leap, ye lame, for joy.

I'd always sung the verse as if it were addressed to others: the deaf, the speechless, the blind, the lame—people with whom I could rejoice but not personally identify. But this time the Spirit flashed a phrase directly at me: "Your loosened tongue employ."

The rest of the worshipers finished off the song, but I stopped short, taking in a two-pronged reminder: first, I could not take the credit for having "loosened" my own tongue. The turnaround had come as a gift of God. Second, having given that gift, the Spirit was challenging me to continue to use it for God's glory and praise.

I now can summarize the Spirit's word by quoting Paul's admonition in 2 Timothy 1:6: "Fan into flame the gift of God." The next verse talks more about the gift and its challenge: "For God did not give us a spirit of timidity, but a spirit of power, of love and of self-discipline." The King James Version gives a slightly different twist: "God hath not given us the spirit of fear; but of power, and of love, and of a sound mind."

Has God "loosened your tongue"? Or given you some new power over some physical or emotional handicap? Accept the challenge. Employ the gift. Then praise the Giver.

❧

Lord, you've set a challenge before me: to fan into flame the gifts you've given me. Accepting that challenge feels risky. I have only one tongue—not a thousand—and only two hands and two feet, but I want to step out in faith. Increase my faith in your sustaining power and love.

Part VII

Hymns as Prayers

He who sings prays twice.
Augustine

Abide with Me

Henry Lyte, 1793 – 1847

Abide with me, fast falls the eventide,
The darkness deepens—Lord, with me abide;
When other helpers fail, and comforts flee,
Help of the helpless, O abide with me.

Swift to its close ebbs out life's little day;
Earth's joys grow dim, its glories pass away;
Change and decay in all around I see;
O thou who changest not, abide with me.

Dusk. It speaks of a potentially threatening transition. In the daytime you can see the enemy. At night, who knows what harm lurks in the dark?

As a child regularly attending Sunday evening services, I learned and liked "Abide with Me." As "the darkness deepened" outside the stained-glass windows, the One "who changest not" would surely stick around. Then there was also the line referring to God as the "Help of the helpless"—which meant the children, of course. Knowing little of consequential "change and decay," I sang a simple song that I later whistled as I walked outside into the dark.

A simple song—so I thought.

"Abide with Me" takes on new significance when you know the prayer was written the day its author, a fifty-four-year-old clergyman, preached his last sermon, forced into "early retirement" by failing lungs. Doctors told Henry Lyte he faced major transitions. Think death. His one hope for prolonged breath was in leaving the damp English seaside and moving to the drier Mediterranean climate. Think Rome.

Lyte had pastored the Anglican church in Brixham, England, for twenty-four years. On September 4, 1847, he said farewell. He preached on Luke 24:29, the text of the resurrected Jesus meeting two disciples on the road to Emmaus; at their request—"Abide with us: for it is toward evening, and the day is far spent" (KJV)—Jesus ate dinner with them. He revealed himself to them. In short, he lingered in their presence.

And the Scripture verse lingered in Lyte's thoughts. Late that afternoon he walked across his garden to the familiar seashore, where the prayer-poem took shape: a request that Christ would stay near through an imminent, difficult night.

Come dusk, Lyte went to his room and wrote out eight stanzas and also a melody, now lost.

Lyte never reached sunny Italy. He died en route in November in Nice, France. His hand reaching toward the sky, he whispered, "Peace, joy," and lost his breath—that last transition seeming as easy as he had hoped—as "heaven's morning" broke through.

"Abide with Me." To a child it's a song to whistle in the dark. To someone facing death its prayer requests the Lord to stay near—to reveal his changeless self even in the midst of change that marks the ultimate physical decay.

To most of us, living somewhere between the morning and evening of life, the song invites the Lord to walk with us through any number of transitions that prompt us to wonder what awaits us—beyond the change. Our qualms can be calmed in another prayer, spoken by Jesus himself as he faced his earthly farewell. "I will pray the Father, and he shall give you another Comforter, that he may abide with you for ever" (John

14:16 KJV). Here Jesus asks the Father to send the Spirit—to abide with us disciples—forever. And that means through the transition. He abides.

❧

Lord, I need your presence, every hour of every day. I pray that you will dwell with me as I walk through the transitions—some as predictable as dusk and some that come by surprise and overwhelm me. In life and when I face death, Lord, abide.

Just as I Am

Charlotte Elliott, 1789 - 1871

Just as I am, without one plea,
But that thy blood was shed for me,
And that thou bidd'st me come to thee,
O Lamb of God, I come! I come!

Charlotte Elliott—granddaughter, daughter, sister, and niece to a grand line of pious Anglican clergymen—wrote the words to this song after having been an invalid some twelve years. Shortly after her health failed, she had become a believer at the urging of a man who had said, "You must come to Christ just as you are." Before you've tidied yourself up. Before you've worked out your own salvation.

Years later, feeling particularly useless and "invalid" when everyone in her parsonage home was rushing around preparing for a church-school fund-raising bazaar, those words came back to Elliott. By the end of the event, she had written *the* invitational hymn of the twentieth century. *Come to God. Not later. But today. Now.*

Like Elliott, my friend Jack was born into a family known for its generational piety. But as an adolescent Jack tuned out the altar calls. Then he more blatantly rebelled, leaving the church behind.

He thought he'd shaken off the God bit, until, in 1980, his wife turned a corner—reading her Bible, returning to church, quietly living out a new faith.

Jack? He was bemused by changes in her demeanor and behavior. But as for faith—he knew better. The concept of God was irrational, nonsensical. God didn't exist.

But in time his wife's witness won a hearing. Jack went with her to church. Once. He returned occasionally, and a pattern developed: he would enjoy the contemporary music—drums, guitars, the works. He would sit through—mentally criticize—the sermon. At Communion time he followed his wife down the aisle. But at a critical crossroads, the pair parted ways; she turned right toward the altar, and he turned left to escape for a cigarette.

This went on for more than a year, when, for Jack, God started breaking every barrier down. Another pattern developed: Jack would find himself in a fix—in need of divine intervention—and would pose, *If there is really a God, then . . . [an utterly improbable something] will happen.* And it did.

One Saturday this scenario played out twice. The next morning Jack got up for church and felt drawn to receive Communion. He walked forward even as questions remained: Should he receive? Did he really believe? Was God here?

In the aisle, as he neared the crossroads, Jack heard an inner voice laying out an implausible scenario: *If they sing "Just as I Am," you should take Communion.*

Jack smiled. He couldn't imagine they would—this being an *Episcopal* church and one that relied on overhead transparencies (praise songs) not fat hymnbooks (old songs).

But before Jack had taken two steps, the band led the congregation in three mournful, unmistakable notes. The words? "Just as I am, without one plea. . . ."

Jack heard the same inner voice: *You can no longer say I am not here. You can go left, and I will leave you alone, or you can go right and come to me.*

Suddenly the cigarette wasn't terribly important.

"Just as I am, and waiting not...." When Charlotte Elliott published this and other poems in *The Invalid's Hymn Book* (1834), she printed the six stanzas along with Jesus' promise in John 6:37: "Him that cometh to me I will in no wise cast out" (KJV).

And that promise still stands as a universal invitation to all to receive his saving, cleansing grace. No matter what you are. Who you are. Where you are. You are welcome, like Jack, to turn right and receive.

Lord, just as I am, I come in faith that you will receive me—welcome, pardon, cleanse, and relieve me of my heavy load.

Dear Lord and Father of Mankind

John Greenleaf Whittier, 1807 – 92

Dear Lord and Father of mankind,
Forgive our foolish ways!
Reclothe us in our rightful mind,
In purer lives thy service find,
In deeper reverence praise.

There's no mistaking—Mr. Whittier had a point of view: that God speaks in whispers and delights in those who listen well and respond with ordered reverence and service.

John Greenleaf Whittier was a deeply committed Christian of conviction, a journalist, editor, and poet who heralded the cause of abolition. He did not listen only to absorb and hoard the message. But listen he did. As a New England Quaker he attended silent services—no singing, no prepared sermon—waiting for the Holy Spirit to speak to the human spirit.

Whittier's theology and temperament left little room for any wild-eyed whooping. Reports of a local, feverish camp meeting seem to have prompted his writing a seventeen-stanza poem ("The Brewing of Soma") that ends with this solemn prayer: "Dear Lord and Father of mankind, forgive."

Soma was an ancient Hindu hallucinogenic potion brewed and blessed as the "drink of the gods." The effects were otherworldly: religious frenzy and altered states of mind. Whittier described partakers who "soared upward, with strange joy elate" but when "sobered sank to earth."

Whittier didn't leave the Hindu priests alone in their delusions; there was that camp meeting down the road.

> *And yet the past comes round again,*
> > *And new doth old fulfil;*
> *In sensual transports, wild as vain,*
> *We brew in many a Christian fane*
> > *The heathen Soma still.*

For this Whittier pled heaven's mercy and humanity's remorse.

Twelve years after the poem was published in *Atlantic Monthly,* a hymnal editor pulled the closing "Dear Lord" prayer from its original context and let it speak for itself. Like God at a Quaker meeting.

The words still speak. You with ears, do you hear?

Whittier knew his Bible, at least selectively (like any of us, though we might not admit it); this hymn-prayer is laden with biblical images.

Verse 1 refers to a healed demoniac who presented himself "dressed and in his right mind" (Mark 5:15).

Verse 2 asks that we remember the "simple trust" of the disciples who "without a word" responded to Jesus' call: "Follow me."

The last verse takes us to Mount Horeb and God's message to Elijah—heard not in the flashy "earthquake, wind, and fire" but in the whisper of a "still small voice of calm" (1 Kings 19:11–12).

Unfortunately American hymnals consistently drop one verse, a deletion that leaves verse 3 dangling and confusing:

> *O Sabbath rest by Galilee!*
> > *O calm of hills above,*

Where Jesus knelt to share with thee
The silence of eternity,
 Interpreted by love!

In his original scheme Whittier finished the thought:

With that deep hush subduing all
 Our words and works that drown
The tender whisper of thy call,
As noiseless let thy blessing fall
 As fell thy manna down.

Stop. Look. Listen. This is Whittier's driving theme: Our striving words and works can drown out the Father's whisper. Upon discovering this "lost" Whittier stanza (in a Scottish hymnal), one pastor reflected on his ministry: "In years past I acted in a way that said that if the world were going to be saved from hell, the responsibility lay on my shoulders.

"I now see that God wants to pour out his blessing, on us and on his world, not through our feverish activity—our 'striving, strain, and stress'—but through his quiet ways. Our busyness actually prevents us from hearing 'the tender whisper of thy call.' What God is doing at any moment far overshadows the importance of what I am doing. My ministry will be most effective when I first sense what God is doing and then seek to move with him."

Stop. Look. Listen. For a brief time don't even search for a song to sing. Just listen. Hear the word of the Lord. The whisper. Shh.

"Be still, and know that I am God" (Psalm 46:10).

Drop thy still dews of quietness,
 Till all our striving cease;
Take from our souls the strain and stress,
And let our ordered lives confess
 The beauty of thy peace.

Breathe through the heats of our desire
Thy coolness and thy balm;
Let sense be dumb, let flesh retire;
Speak through the earthquake, wind, and fire,
O still small voice of calm!

Spirit of God, Descend upon My Heart

George Croly, 1780 - 1860

Spirit of God, descend upon my heart;
Wean it from earth, through all its pulses move;
Stoop to my weakness, mighty as thou art,
And make me love thee as I ought to love.

At fortysomething, it's hard for me to comprehend the bond between a teenaged girl and her high school ring. I say that with dispassion, and yet just two years ago I wrote a pointed poem titled "Why I Was Not Allowed to Buy a High School Ring." After twenty years I still retained the pain of the prohibition.

Jane Campbell, coauthor of *Growing Up Born Again*, vividly remembers the trauma of losing such a treasured ring— cut a bit too large—months before her high school graduation. "I was beside myself," she says, with passion. She searched. Prayed. Then repeated the pattern and tried both at once.

Months passed, and the lost ring was never far below the level of her conscious mind. And thoughts of the ring surfaced, front and center, during a Sunday morning church service. "We sang 'Spirit of God, Descend upon My Heart,'" she recalls.

Though the melody flows gracefully, anyone, teenaged or middle-aged, could easily stumble through the first difficult stanzas of poetry by George Croly, bespeaking surrender to God. But for Jane that day, the message was clear. And from the bottom of the fourth verse, a memorable line ascended and attached itself to her lost ring: "Teach me the patience of unanswered prayer." The request was itself a prayer that Jane allowed herself to sing and then dwell on: *God, teach me your ways. I know you've heard my prayer. Now I'm waiting on you—with patience.*

Jane says, "I'd flitted along through my school years, doing the right Christian things. This was one of first times I knew God had given me a message, and I responded" with a willing spirit.

And so did God. An hour later, setting the table for the family dinner, Jane found her ring, resting secure in a drawer of the dining-room hutch.

Jane knows the truth of Ecclesiastes 7:8: "The end of a matter is better than its beginning, / and patience is better than pride." She says, "To have an answer come within hours—after the ring had been lost for months—the message was clear: that God was there and intervening in my life." And waiting patiently to teach a lesson in patience.

A high school ring is probably not the treasure you're waiting to reclaim. No matter what your loss, allow yourself to pray the submission prayer penned by Croly, a hardworking pastor of a London-slum Anglican parish.

Spirit of God, descend upon my heart and make me teachable. Show me how to check the doubts that rise . . . the rebel sighs. Teach me the patience of unanswered prayer, even as I make my heart an altar enflamed by your love.

How Great Thou Art

Stuart K. Hine, 1899 – 1989

O Lord my God! When I in awesome wonder
Consider all the worlds Thy hands have made,
I see the stars, I hear the rolling thunder,
Thy power throughout the universe displayed.
Then sings my soul, my Saviour God to Thee:
How great Thou art! How great Thou art![†]

How Great Thou Art" has been recorded by a wide range of musicians—from Elvis Presley to Lawrence Welk and company. But for many the song seems synonymous with one singer, George Beverly Shea, who "introduced" it in a Toronto Billy Graham Crusade in 1955.

But its history predates that event. The first line was inspired by a Swedish poem "O Store Gud" ("O Great God"), written in 1886 by a lay preacher and parliamentarian, Carl Boberg. Once translated into Russian, the poem was set to the melody of an old Swedish folk song, which we recognize as "How Great Thou Art."

[†]Copyright 1953 by S. K. Hine. Assigned to Manna Music, Inc., 35255 Brooten Road, Pacific City, OR 97135. Renewed 1981. All rights reserved. Used by permission. The author's original words are "works" in place of "worlds" and "mighty" in place of "rolling."

In 1927 Stuart Hine, a British missionary in Eastern Europe, discovered the Russian song. Inspired by the folk tune and the opening line, he wrote his own hymn of praise. It's not surprising that Hine's poetic muse initially struck during a storm—thunder rolling across the Carpathian Mountains. The second verse was inspired as Hine later tromped through the woods with a group of young people. He wrote the third verse in response to the conversion of a number of people.

During World War II, back in Britain, Hine added a fourth verse. Through publication in a missionary magazine and then printed leaflets, the hymn found a worldwide audience. And in London in 1954, a book publisher handed one of those leaflets to George Beverly Shea, saying, "Here is something you might like to sing."

The song became one of Shea's trademarks, evident in the title of his autobiography, *Then Sings My Soul*. With some amazement and amusement he there notes that "I sang 'How Great Thou Art' with the choir a total of ninety-nine times" in conjunction with the 1957 New York City Billy Graham Crusade.

Shea continues, "Singing any number that often can sometimes cause us to lose the full impact of the words. I remember one night toward the end of the Madison Square Garden meeting when my weariness got the best of me. I caught myself mouthing the words rather than singing them from the heart."

Later, in his room, Shea felt the Spirit's tug, reminding him not to take lightly the hymn's message. That night he prayed, asking forgiveness for his "apathy in singing that great hymn" and promising that it wouldn't happen again.[1]

One needn't be a professional singer to slip into that robotic mode, uttering phrases with little thought to their meaning.

Next time you catch yourself tuning out as you sing praises, stop. Hear it again as if it were the first time. Wonder the wow. "How Great Thou Art."

Lord, when I'm tired or careless and slip into a mindless mode, mouthing empty words of praise, send me a reminder of your greatness. Open my eyes to the wonder of your creation. Make me pause and consider anew how great you truly are. Awesome. With the psalmist I pray: "I will praise you, O Lord my God, with all my heart" (Psalm 86:12).

Come, Thou Fount of Every Blessing

Robert Robinson, 1735 – 90

Come, thou Fount of every blessing
Tune my heart to sing thy grace;
Streams of mercy, never ceasing,
Call for songs of loudest praise. . . .

O to grace how great a debtor
Daily I'm constrained to be!
Let that grace, Lord like a fetter,
Bind my wandering heart to thee:
Prone to wander, Lord, I feel it,
Prone to leave the God I love;
Take my heart, O take and seal it,
Seal it for thy courts above.

As a teenager Robert Robinson was up to no good. Fatherless, apprenticed to a London barber, he fell in with the wrong crowd, what we would call a gang. One Sunday when he was seventeen, he and friends tried to get an old fortune-teller drunk, intending to get free fortunes and make sport of her tales.

But actually the woman's prophecy—that Robinson would live to see his children and grandchildren—gave him pause. *Is my reckless life what I want for my children?* That night he was further sobered by a sermon he had meant to mock: the great revivalist George Whitefield preaching on Matthew 3:7, "O generation of vipers, who hath warned you to flee from the wrath to come?" (KJV). Robinson's notebooks say he found God that night, but it was three more years before he felt inner peace or the joy of his salvation.

At age twenty-three, now a pastor himself, Robinson wrote "Come, Thou Fount" for Pentecost, the celebration of the coming of the Holy Spirit. Robinson's hymn includes an odd mix of metaphors, from fluid waterflows to restricting fetters. The beseeching prayer starts on a note of gratitude for God's streams of mercy and ends with a faith-filled plea for that grace to bind a heart prone to wander. (See Hosea 11:2, 4: "The more I called Israel, / the further they went from me. . . . / I led them with cords of human kindness, / with ties of love.")

In my informal survey, asking Christians if they've been touched by a specific hymn, a New York actor quoted one line of Robinson's last verse: "Prone to wander, Lord, I feel it." He gave no details; he was just aware of the truth of the phrase, and acknowledging the tug that would pull him away from the Fount was itself a fetter that tethered him close.

That lesson may have been lost on the hymn's writer. It's told that in his later years, though still a pastor, Robinson grew careless in his Christian walk, losing the close communion with God he had once enjoyed. On a stagecoach one day, a fellow passenger read aloud the words to "Come, Thou Fount." In persistent conversation, she asked Robinson his opinion of the poem.

Caught up short by the very lines he'd written, Robinson grew teary eyed and quietly replied, "Madam, I am the poor, unhappy man who composed it; and I would give a thousand worlds, if I had them, to enjoy the feelings I had then." In wandering adrift, he had lost his joy. To find it again? He didn't need to give the thousand worlds that weren't his; he needed only to walk back into the Fount, gushing on and on, as constant as time.

Tempted to wander? Admit that you're part of the human race—in need of the Spirit's empowering grace, a tether to the Fount of every blessing.

Lord, when I'm tempted to wander, remind me of the image of your grace being a fetter made of love. Draw me close. Bind my heart to you.

$\mathcal{L}$ead, Kindly Light

John Henry Newman, 1801 – 90

Lead, kindly Light, amid the encircling gloom,
*   Lead thou me on;*
The night is dark, and I am far from home,
*   Lead thou me on.*

$\mathcal{A}$ny number of hymns can be condensed into three words: *Lord, lead me.* There's "Lead Me, Guide Me"; "Father, Lead Me Day by Day"; "Lead On, O King Eternal"; "He Leadeth Me"; "Savior, Like a Shepherd Lead Us". . . .

"Lead, Kindly Light" may be the most difficult to navigate, musically and poetically. (It is not included in many current hymnals; having written a poem, not a hymn, author John Henry Newman thought the text quite unsingable and was bemused by the song's great popularity.) The second and third verses border on scratch-your-head-huh? poetic mystery. But the first verse redeems the remainder. The message is clear and universally understood: "The night is dark, and I am far from home."

When he wrote this poem, thirty-three-year-old Newman was one homesick man.

In December 1832, he set out on his first international voyage, a sabbatical from his pastoral duties at an Anglican church in Oxford. Distressed by various ecclesiastical, cultural, and political trends, Newman's health had dimmed. A friend had suggested a Mediterranean respite—and the two men set sail for Italy and Sicily. Staying on longer than his friend, Newman contracted a virulent virus, which thrust him to the brink of death. He later noted that during this sickness he felt a strong but undefined call on his life. He assured his servant-nurse, "I shall not die. . . . God has a work for me to do in England."

But what was the task? Newman wasn't sure; his vision was blocked—and yet he remained expectant. His mind-set seems framed in one daily ritual: when recuperating in Italy, he would wake before dawn and wait for the sun to rise. With the first rays he would mutter, "O sweet light! God's best gift."

Once recovered enough to travel back to England, he still had to wait for a ship that could take him on. "I was aching to get home," he admitted. Finally in June he booked passage on a boat loaded with oranges, sailing north to Marseilles.

Newman had been "on holiday" for six months; he was ready to get on with life—whatever that would mean—but he still faced obstacles. Once offshore, the orange boat—and weak-kneed Newman—sat in the treacherous strait between Corsica and Sicily for a steamy week—waiting for wind to lift the sails and the fog. And there, on an oppressive Sunday in 1833, Newman wrote his prayerful request:

> *Lead, kindly Light, amid the encircling gloom . . .*
> *Keep thou my feet; I do not ask to see*
> *The distant scene; one step enough for me.*

Like most great poems, Newman's works on more than one level. Is he reflecting his helplessness at being physically sick and lost and blocked in, desperate to get home? It seems. Is he spiritually groping, fogged in, unsure of the road ahead? It seems. (Before leaving Oxford he had said he felt as if he were being "led on by God's hand blindly, not knowing whither he is taking me.")

Whether the plea for guidance was physical or spiritual, the prayer was answered. The boat sailed safely into the

Atlantic; on July 9, Newman greeted his mother in England. And the very next Sunday Newman heard a sermon from his own pulpit that set in motion the Oxford Movement—the "task" that would capture Newman's energies and talents for twelve years, until he joined the Catholic Church and accepted a new call, eventually being named cardinal.

Look again at Newman's prayer and the depth of faith it calls forth when one is "far from home" and forced into a "holding pattern." Where is the gentle wind to blow off the fog? Where is the kind light to show the way?

It's a prayer of faith and expectation that one can make one's own: *I'm a long way from where I want to be, and it's dark out here. Lord, enlighten the path that leads me home. But "I do not ask to see / The distant scene; one step [is] enough for me." I'm willing to take one step at a time in the right direction; I look to you to show me where to place my foot.*

*L*ord, *I condense my prayer to four words: Lead me, kindly, please.*

Part VIII

Songs
of Testimony

My life flows on in endless song,
above earth's lamentation; . . .
It sounds an echo in my soul;
how can I keep from singing?

Traditional Quaker Song

A Wonderful Savior Is Jesus My Lord

Fanny Crosby, 1820 – 1915

He hideth my soul in the cleft of the rock
That shadows a dry, thirsty land;
He hideth my life in the depths of his love,
And covers me there with his hand.

This summer my brother drove across the Rockies, taking time to enjoy the scenery. He says the sight of a deep cleft in a huge rock reminded him of this song written by Fanny Crosby.

Having seen at least the Front Range—and awesome nature film footage—I could appreciate his description. And then I stopped short, realizing the song had been written by a woman who had been blind from infancy. What was her understanding of being hidden in the cleft of a rock?

Actually, we know virtually nothing about the circumstances of the writing of these lyrics. Crosby churned out some nine thousand songs, many commissioned to fit a particular tune, many deservedly forgotten.

But this one remains in hymnals and in hearts. Providing assurance . . . even building bridges over deep ravines.

Robert McIntyre of Marion, Indiana, tells of pastoring a church as a young man. His denomination valued the voice of the laity—to the point that once a year a congregation voted by ballot: do we want to retain or release the current pastor? Majority ruled—though many thin-skinned pastors resigned, disgraced by just a hint of discontent.

Having pastored the slowly growing church for several years, Robert received the disconcerting news that he'd received a "call to stay"—but by a slim margin. Thin-skinned or not, he says, "a vote like that is not a good base for continuing constructive ministry." But "as I considered my response, I learned what had happened." The chair of the committee overseeing the vote had canvassed the membership, urging everyone to vote for change. Her reason? In Robert's words: "'Our pastor has too much education. We need someone like ——.' Whereupon she would name a minister with virtually the same education as mine."

Robert sought the counsel of his district supervisor, who advised him not to resign. "That kind of activity should not be permitted to succeed."

Easy for him to say.

But Robert girded up his loins and stayed another year.

That summer, he admits, "I could not help but feel a tension toward the sister who had attempted the coup."

Then, one seemingly ordinary Sunday, he led the congregation as they sang a song that had no obvious connection to the political discord. Nothing about church unity or forgiveness or being truehearted. Just the refreshing words of "He Hideth My Soul."

> *A wonderful Savior is Jesus my Lord,*
> *He taketh my burden away;*
> *He holdeth me up, and I shall not be moved,*
> *He giveth me strength as my day.*
> *He hideth my soul in the cleft of the rock*
> *That shadows a dry, thirsty land;*
> *He hideth my life in the depths of his love,*
> *And covers me there with his hand.*

But the Spirit used the song—this particular verse—to build the bridge that spanned the gulf between pastor and parishioner.

Buttressed by and enfolded in the love of God, Robert felt compelled "to step down from the platform and shake hands with members of the congregation, including 'the sister' in the second pew. (This was before the days of hugging in church.) Tears flowed freely. The tension (at least on my part) was gone."

Robert had several options in this difficult time. He could have carried gruff resentment on his shoulder. He could have ducked behind cars and into closets to avoid awkward encounters. But gracious community was restored—not as Robert vindicated himself or as he ran away but as he allowed himself to seek the refreshing shelter of the Savior, who gives strength, who upholds those who turn to him.

There was no human engineering behind this transformation of heart. Just God at work as someone was willing to let him.

I expect that's the way it was with Fanny Crosby—writing a song about a mountain crag when she'd never seen one. God at work, whispering to a heart.

In *Unspoken Sermons* George Macdonald poses a parishioner's question that might be Robert's or Fanny's or yours: "But how can God bring this about in me?"

Macdonald's response speaks still: "Let him do it, and perhaps you will know how."

❧

Lord, sometimes I'm aware only of the things I should do for you. Today open my eyes to things I've never seen before. Give me new insight regarding the innumerable things you do for me—the ways you crown my moments with blessing. Being my Savior. Taking my burdens away. Holding me up. Giving me strength. Transforming my heart.

I Know Whom I Have Believed

Daniel W. Whittle, 1840 – 1901

I know not why God's wondrous grace
To me he hath made known,
Nor why—unworthy—Christ in love
Redeemed me for his own.

But "I know whom I have believed,
And am persuaded that he is able
To keep that which I've committed
Unto him against that day."

I find two versions of the spiritual conversion of Daniel Whittle, eventually one of a host of writers who fed the Dwight Moody evangelistic era with an ample supply of gospel songs.

One conversion story claims Whittle found God during the Civil War. Captured and held in a Confederate prison, he started to read the New Testament his mother had handed him three years before when he had joined the Union army. (The other account details a pre-War rebirth in the womblike setting of a walk-in vault at a Chicago Wells Fargo Bank where he was employed.)

Major Whittle, as he came to be known after being decorated as a hero, didn't write "I Know Whom I Have Believed" until 1883, when he was a popular traveling evangelist. The song's five verses show some originality, but the repeating refrain is taken directly from the King James translation of 2 Timothy 1:12.

And that refrain makes me prefer the war-story conversion: a parent's faith and action having a direct impact on a son or daughter.

This preference is tied to the significance Whittle's song holds for one mother, named Dorotha. Her children are grown and parents, even grandparents, themselves. But, she says, "when they were teenagers and rebelling or coming home with problems, I would sing and sing 'I Know Whom I Have Believed,' especially one line: '[I] am persuaded that he is able to keep that which I've committed unto him. . . .' I had committed my children to him—as babies and then every day—and I chose to believe that he would 'keep' them."

That Scripture song steadied Dorotha's perspective, kept her faith focused on what God was able to do, as she continually committed her life and offspring to him. And God was faithful. She now boasts of her youngest great-grandchild, born to missionary parents.

You see why I like the story of Mother Whittle sending her son off to war, a prayer on her lips, a Bible in his pack, a legacy that would lead to his own salvation and to a confident testimony that would encourage other parents for generations.

Writing about Whittle's song has sent me to 2 Timothy 1, to read the context of the emphatic "I am persuaded that God is able to keep." The passage continues, in somewhat circular fashion urging readers themselves to "keep" (guard) "the good thing" (KJV) committed to them: "Guard the good deposit that was entrusted to you—guard it with the help of the Holy Spirit."

The Scripture isn't talking about parents guarding children, but the parallel seems appropriate, and I challenge you to team up with God as you raise—and eventually release—the children entrusted to you: Commit your children to him. Be persuaded that he is able to keep them. In faith look to the Spirit for help as together you guard the younger generation—your faith being a shield to protect their journey to their eternal home.

⌒

Lord, increase my faith as I daily commit my children—young or grown—to your keeping. Guide their steps. Guard their path. Draw them to yourself.

My Jesus, as Thou Wilt

Benjamin Schmolk, 1672 – 1737
trans. by Jane Borthwick

My Jesus, as thou wilt; O may thy will be mine!
Into thy hand of love I would my all resign;
Through sorrow or through joy
Conduct me as thine own,
And help me still to say,
"My Lord, thy will be done."

This hymn is tied to one particular melody, taken from a wordless opera overture composed by Carl Maria von Weber, who reportedly died after uttering, "Let me go back to my own home and then God's will be done." It seems the lyrics and tune were wed some years later. Did the hymn arranger consciously connect the composer with the text?

The answer is lost, as are the specifics of the writing of the German text in 1709. But we do know something of the life circumstances of Benjamin Schmolk. This pastor-poet walked a precarious political tightrope. After Luther's breakaway Reformation, the Roman Catholic Church had swept its own house, staging a Counter-Reformation. In a day when church and state were intertwined, by treaty specific districts were tagged—some as Catholic, some as Lutheran.

Here's the rub: Schmolk pastored the only legal Lutheran church in the formerly Protestant but now declared Catholic district of Silesia. Under rigid restrictions, one small wood-framed church served thirty-six villages. A steeple? *Verboten*. A bell? *Nein*. Schmolk was even forbidden to serve Communion to a sick or dying parishioner unless he first received special permission from the Catholic priest.

And yet for thirty-five years he faithfully worked as pastor, serving his people as best he could, even after a stroke immobilized his right hand.

This is the man who at age thirty-seven wrote an eleven-stanza poem—"My Jesus, as Thou Wilt"—that has been described as a hymn of resignation.

Maybe. But resigned to what? He didn't exactly give up the fight. Life and mission was too dear to lie down and wait for death.

This hymn has become a life theme for Priscilla Andrews. As unlikely as it sounds, back in the fifties a group of hearty eighteen-year-olds voted this their college class song. Priscilla among them.

Once she graduated, the somber tune rarely crossed her mind until thirty years later, when a doctor discovered colon cancer. The hymn-prayer came to mind as she lay in a hospital bed, weak, in pain, and traumatized by the drastic surgery that had, digestively speaking, shut down the main north-south line. Rerouted the traffic. No temporary measure. A permanent, utterly inconvenient detour. For as long as life would last—but on that count no long-term guarantees.

In the first days of recuperating and in the months and years that have followed—through one recurrence—Priscilla has chosen to walk her own tightrope. While resigning herself to God's will—claiming Schmolk's hymn as her theme, requesting that it be sung at her funeral, whenever that may be—she has chosen to fight with all she has for life. Which God has granted, with health and vitality.

There's power in Schmolk's hymn because he lays out a resignation that is framed in the context of a hopeful future.

> Let not my star of hope
> Grow dim or disappear . . .
>
> Each changing future scene
> I gladly trust with thee . . .

Grounded in such a faith, we, like Christ himself, can ". . . sing in life or death, 'My Lord, thy will be done.'"

Lord, I frequently recite your model prayer: "Your will be done on earth, as it is in heaven." Help me to better understand what that prayer means. Help me to rest in your will even as I put one foot in front of the other and run the race you've set before me.

And Can It Be?

Charles Wesley, 1707 - 88

And can it be that I should gain
An interest in the Savior's blood?
Died he for me, who caused his pain?
For me, who him to death pursued?
Amazing love! How can it be
That thou, my God, shouldst die for me?

And Can It Be?" is a conversion testimony that has grown more popular in recent years—and this despite its daunting first verse, which is difficult both grammatically and theologically.

This song relates the conversion story of an okay guy, not your typical loathsome wretch. Wesley was the son of a preacher, an Oxford graduate, an ordained Anglican clergyman, a world traveler—having spent five months in the New World colony of Georgia as secretary and chaplain to Gov. James Oglethorpe. Though he knew about God—and something of "the world"—he did not *know* God or the freedom that comes when God releases one's spirit from bondage. Something primal was missing, until May 21, 1738.

It was Pentecost Sunday. A sick Wesley was the houseguest of an uneducated but spiritually astute Mr. Bray of London. Charles had been reading writings of Martin Luther, the proponent of salvation by grace through faith, not by righteous deeds. Wesley's journal tells the story:

> At midnight I gave myself up to Christ: assured I was safe, sleeping or waking. Had continued experience of his power to overcome all temptations; and confessed, with joy and surprise, that he was able to do exceedingly abundantly for me, above what I can ask or think.
>
> I now found myself at peace with God, and rejoiced in hope of loving Christ. Under his protection I waked next morning, and rejoiced in reading the 107th Psalm, so nobly describing what God had done for my soul.
>
> At nine I began [to write] a hymn on my conversion but was persuaded to break off for fear of pride. Mr. Bray coming, encouraged me to proceed in spite of Satan. I prayed to Christ to stand by me and I finished the hymn

—the first of some six thousand he would pen.

Some scholars think this cited conversion hymn was "Where Shall My Wondering Soul Begin?" (better known in Britain than in the States). But others give clear arguments for it being "And Can It Be?"—which was surely an early hymn, as it was published by year-end.

Three days after Charles's conversion, his brother John similarly gave himself to Christ while attending a Moravian meeting. "I felt my heart strangely warmed," he wrote of his surrender.

With several friends in tow, John barged in on Charles, still recuperating, and announced, "I believe!" And then, Charles reported, "We sang the hymn with great joy." "The hymn" is presumably the testimony of amazement written earlier in the week:

> *Amazing love! How can it be*
> *That thou, my God, shouldst die for me?*

Long my imprisoned spirit lay
Fast bound in sin and nature's night . . .
My chains fell off, my heart was free,
I rose, went forth, and followed thee.

Even a man previously committed to a life of Christian service needed to admit that he was spiritually bound in a dark prison, until the atoning work of Christ broke through the barriers, until Wesley reached out to accept the freedom freely offered. (It's a freedom described in Psalm 107—the psalm Charles read the morning after his conversion: "He brought them out of darkness and the deepest gloom / and broke away their chains" [v. 14].)

One popular camp-meeting evangelist makes dramatic use of this song: The congregation sings while seated until they get to this phrase of deliverance: "My chains fell off." Then they jump to their feet and raise their arms, with physical gestures declaring their freedom. The chains are unbound.

In the privacy of your devotional hour, why not act out the play? (That's not to suggest that the freedom offered in Christ is simply melodrama.)

Reach for the freedom offered in Christ. If you've already claimed it, then reclaim and proclaim it.

How can it be?

Through Christ, it is.

❧

*L*ord, *make me newly amazed at the wonder of your love for me.*

In the Cross
of Christ I Glory

Sir John Bowring, 1792 – 1872

In the cross of Christ I glory,
Towering o'er the wrecks of time;
And the light of sacred story
Gathers round its head sublime.

*L*ike "And Can It Be?" this song has a clear, crisp message—if you can get past the first verse.

Legend claims the initial lines describe a literal scene: in Macao, near Hong Kong, John Bowring visited ruins of a cathedral destroyed by fire; only the front wall remained intact—boasting a large metal cross towering over the wreckage. To Bowring, a learned, urbane man, the enduring testimony spoke of larger issues.

This story makes the song easier to get into; it makes concrete Bowring's symbolic picture of the history of humanity—devastation needing the redemptive work of Christ.

Unfortunately historians say the tale's not true; the hymn was published in 1825, decades before Bowring traveled to the Pacific Rim—as British consul to Canton, China, and eventually as an ill-fated governor of Hong Kong.

In the preface to *Hymns,* the book that first contained this song, Bowring wrote:

I have often witnessed with delight the consoling influence produced by the recollection of some passage of devotional poetry.... Should any fragment of this little book, remembered in moments of gloom and anxiety, tend to restore peace, awaken fortitude, create or strengthen confidence in heaven, I shall have obtained the boon for which I pray.[1]

After its opening panorama, "In the Cross" gets personal, and here it touches a responsive chord. First we see the Cross as it relates to hard times in a believer's life:

When the woes of life o'ertake me,
Hopes deceive, and fears annoy,
Never shall the cross forsake me;
Lo! it glows with peace and joy.

My dad tells me this verse sustained him as he drove across snowy New York State twenty years ago "fearing the worst, realizing that some of my hopes might never be realized"; he was responding to a "you'd better come, immediately" call from a hospital treating my younger brother, critically injured in an auto accident. My brother recovered, though the road was long, and my father has since been able to turn to Bowring's next verse—the Cross and its effect on better days:

When the sun of bliss is beaming
Light and love upon my way,
From the cross the radiance streaming
Adds more luster to the day.

Then Bowring turns to the "mix" that makes for real life:

Bane and blessing, pain and pleasure,
By the cross are sanctified;
Peace is there that knows no measure,
Joys that through all time abide.

In the end Bowring brings us back to the abiding story of *time*. But not as a wreckage; here it is sanctified, a journey that can be marked by peace despite pain and joy that endures. Because what ultimately matters is what happened on the towering old cross.

Sir Bowring's purposeful prayer was answered. His song does "strengthen confidence in heaven."

Cling to Christ, let him redeem the days of your life, the woes and bliss, the whole whopping story.

Lord, the apostle Paul's prayer (Galatians 6:14) is mine: "May I never boast [glory] except in the cross of our Lord Jesus Christ, through which the world has been crucified to me, and I to the world." Help me to cling to the Cross and its redemptive work in my life.

O Jesus, I Have Promised

John Ernest Bode, 1816 – 74

O Jesus, I have promised
To serve thee to the end;
Be thou forever near me,
My Master and my Friend.

An Anglican clergyman, John Bode wrote this testimony of intent for the confirmation service of his daughter and two sons—the original poem (titled "A Hymn for the Newly Confirmed") reading "O Jesus, we have promised."

The bold beginning of this hymn reminds me of a camp-meeting testimony one never hears anymore: "I'm going to go all the way with Jesus." *I'm going to be faithful to the end, till I die; God and you-all can count on me, come hail or high water.*

It also draws me to the gospel story of Peter's brash claim that he would never deny his Lord: "Even if all fall away on account of you, I never will" (Matthew 26:33).

But as I take a closer look at Bode's pledge of fidelity, it does seem less rash than Peter's. Only four of Bode's original forty-eight lines describe "my promise" as opposed to God's provision. Its bravado is tamed by its humble request for help. *God, I promise to serve you—to the end. And you—be at my side; be my guide and guardian; let me feel you; let me hear you.*

Two "let me see you" verses are consistently deleted from our hymnals. One of these refers to Jesus' response to Peter's broken promise.

> *O let me see . . .*
> *The look that beamed on Peter*
> *When he thy name denied;*
> *The look that draws thy loved ones*
> *Close to thy pierced side.*

Lord, if I stumble, if I'm not faithful on some count, gently tug me back to and through repentance.

Peter didn't keep his rash promise. But his fall didn't keep him from making a more reasonable claim a week later, after Christ's resurrection. As the disciples finished a seaside breakfast, Jesus fired a question directly at a humbled Peter: "Do you truly love me?"

"Yes, Lord."

Then "take care of my sheep" (John 21:16). *Then get up. We're going to keep walking—to the end. Follow me; serve me.* In this conversation Jesus even gave Peter a hint of what his "end" was to be—a martyr's murder.

And empowered by the Spirit, Peter remained faithful. He saw his service through.

For his children—and for us—Bode explains how:

> *My hope to follow duly*
> *Is in thy strength alone.*

As I first looked at "O Jesus, I Have Promised," I saw it as a presumptuous testimony of intent. *Oh, be careful little tongue what you promise.* But I have softened my view. Thanks to Jesus' redemptive response to a bumbling Peter. Thanks to Bode's graceful lines. I can see why it has been ranked high in polls of "favorite hymns." I can see why it was recently sung at a funeral, as a testimony to the life of a generous, committed woman. She had made and by grace kept the promise.

And Jesus I have promised
To serve thee to the end;
O give me grace to follow,
My Master and my Friend.

And in the end, she had staked a claim:

O Jesus, thou hast promised
To all who follow thee
That where thou art in glory
There shall thy servant be.

O guide me, call me, draw me,
Uphold me to the end;
And then in heaven receive me,
My Savior and my Friend.

Bode wrote a testimony to live by and die by. A prayer for the young and old. For tomorrow and today. For you and me.

Lord, make this testimony of intent the theme of my life.

There's a Wideness in God's Mercy

Frederick W. Faber, 1814 - 63

There's a wideness in God's mercy,
Like the wideness of the sea;
There's a kindness in his justice,
Which is more than liberty.

It's Monday morning. As I start to write, I pick up a copy of my first book, written fifteen years ago. I haven't read it in years, but I am sure I wrote of a strengthening hymn. Yes, I find the page, describing myself two years out of college and adjusting to a "heavy" job promotion:

> I had received what I felt was a sign that God would see me through the new job. It had come from the pen of Martin Luther, from the hymn "A Mighty Fortress Is Our God," and it was portions of one verse that I repeated when I felt as if I were drowning:
>
> *Did we in our own strength confide,*
> *Our striving would be losing;*
> *Were not the right Man on our side,*
> *The Man of God's own choosing:*
> *...And He must win the battle.*

He, not I, not even the part of my parents that was
in me, was my strength . . . it was God, not a person, who
gave the winning push.[2]

Striving. Fortress. Battle. Winning push. The words speak to a
certain frame of mind. I don't make judgments about the
mind-set. I was young. Where would we be if our callow lost
their mettle? I simply thank God I looked to him for daily
strength.

But this morning I'm overwhelmed with another message, given in another season, midlife. This weekend I smashed
into an emotional abutment; I irrationally overreacted to a simple request: to serve as treasurer of a small organization. "No big
deal," they said, "keeping track of one checkbook."

I said yes. After all, in college I'd tutored accounting students. But upon receiving "the books," I flipped out. Why? To
oversimplify, it brought up old reasons why I never would have
been happy as an accountant. There is no grace in numbers; the
columns are right or wrong. Then there's the irrational leap—
therefore I am right or wrong. Saved or damned.

I didn't sleep well Saturday night. *You've made a commitment you shouldn't break. They're counting on you. . . . But better to
say no now than three months from now. . . . Know and name your
limits. . . . But you should have faith and walk ahead with this. Face
the battle. It's no big deal.*

But it was. It had been a long time since anything had
thrown me into such a dither. Which was the state I was in
when the Sunday morning congregation sang "There's a Wideness in God's Mercy," by Frederick W. Faber. Every word leapt
with meaning:

> *There is no place where earth's sorrows*
> *Are more felt than up in heaven;*
> *There is no place where earth's failings*
> *Have such kindly judgment given.*

> *There is plentiful redemption*
> *In the blood that has been shed;*
> *There is joy for all the members*
> *In the sorrows of the Head.*

This day, the Spirit quickened not a message of strength for the battle (gird up your loins) but one of mercy, kindness, welcome, graces.

The song gained power during an after-church conversation when I called the organization's president—a friend. With not a lot of explanation but with considerable emotion, I quietly pled, "Please, take it away"—the "books," the burden blown out of reasonable proportion.

"Of course, I'll take it away," she said. A wide mercy. Kindly judgment for failings. Healing. An hour later, as I drove to her house to drop off the checkbook, I sang "There's a Wideness" maybe never so aware of what redemption was about: Christ seeing my inadequacies, my wounds, my sins, and saying, "I took it upon myself to take it away from you."

My editor may say that this devotional is too long; that it relates two disparate stories that should be told separately. But I do so to make a point that is at the very heart of this book: we have a God who listens like a mother who can hear a child's breathing suddenly change in the dead of night. We have a God who responds, and not with a prerecorded message. God meets us where we are, and he addresses the needs we face today, in this season. Sometimes we need courage to be Christian soldiers. Sometimes we need comfort, like baby chicks scampering for cover under a mother hen's wings.

God knows our need (even when we don't). And in God we can find the song—the strength—needed for every season.

Today, tomorrow, next year, trust the Spirit to open your heart to a metaphor, a song that shows you direction, strength, and grace for the day. Ask God to speak to your season; hear your heart's cry; widen your view.

For the love of God is broader
Than the measure of the mind;
And the heart of the Eternal
Is most wonderfully kind.

Lord, you know the message I need in this season of my life—
a message that speaks to my needs as it increases my knowledge of you.
I'm listening for the gift of a song. Please put one in my heart.

Part IX

Celebration of Community

Yes, I'll sing the wondrous story
Of the Christ who died for me,
Sing it with the saints in glory,
Gathered by the crystal sea.

Harold Rowley

*L*et Us Break Bread Together

African-American Spiritual

Let us break bread together on our knees,
Let us break bread together on our knees,
When I fall on my knees,
With my face to the rising sun,
O Lord, have mercy on me.

*I*n the last decade "Let Us Break Bread Together" has become one of our favorite Communion hymns—sung by congregants contemplating the mysteries of the Lord's Supper. The first—if not the latter—lines of the spiritual emphasize the communal aspects of the commemoration.

Historians speculate that this black spiritual was not originally a Communion song. It was probably not even sung at a church service. As a "gathering song" it served as a bell to announce an unauthorized meeting of slaves. When some southern states outlawed the more traditional summons—the drumbeat—this song (the original first verse probably being "Let Us Praise God") called a beleaguered community together for communion in every sense of the word.

Communion. What does it mean? The word and its sister, *community,* are rooted in the Latin *communis,* which means "common" as in "participation by all." More than a century of musical and societal evolution has brought this "gathering song" to a fitting place in our worship. At the Lord's Table, we—the communion of saints—have communion with our Lord and with fellow motley members of the church, the body of Christ. As J. B. Phillips has noted: "Holy Communion is surely always falling short of its true purpose if it fails to produce some sense of solidarity with our fellow worshipers."[1] Here at the Lord's Table, let us gather *together* to break bread, drink the cup, and praise and worship God.

In a book of lyrics only (I don't know if the tune is reminiscent of "Let Us Break"), I find a spiritual that introduces an interesting negative into the "Let Us" litany. Read carefully:

> *If we never pray together anymore,*
> *Yes, we'll fall on our knees,*
> *And face the rising sun;*
> *O Lord, have mercy on me.*

> *If we never meet together anymore . . .*
> *If we never groan together anymore . . .*
> *If we never preach together anymore . . .*

Let me add a revised verse:

> *If we never break bread together anymore,*
> *Yes, we'll fall on our knees,*
> *And face the rising sun;*
> *O Lord, have mercy on me.*

If we never gather as one—in solidarity—for Communion, O Lord, have mercy.
On me in my corner.
And you in yours.

Lord, bring me to a new appreciation of the communion of saints that takes place at the Table of our Lord.

The Church's One Foundation

Samuel J. Stone, 1839 – 1900

The church's one Foundation is Jesus Christ her Lord;
She is his new creation by water and the word:
From heaven he came and sought her to be his holy bride;
With his own blood he bought her, and for her life he died.

Sunday after Sunday—even daily as part of their personal devotions—the peasant believers in Windsor, England, recited the ancient formula that outlined the fundamentals of their faith: "I believe in God, the Father almighty, . . . in Jesus Christ, his only Son. . . . I believe in the Holy Spirit, the holy catholic Church, the communion of saints. . . ."

But did they understand what the creed meant? Their young pastor, Samuel Stone, wasn't convinced. As a teaching tool he wrote twelve hymns, each explicating an article of the Apostles' Creed. Hymn 9 delineates characteristics of the universal Christian church and the communion of saints.

That may be the reason Stone wrote "The Church's One Foundation," but it's not why we remember what has been called the great "processional for festivals." (It's the only one of the twelve to have withstood the test of time.) The song, which originally included pointed warnings against heresy, took a stand in a contemporary, newsworthy conflict between Anglicans in South Africa. A conservative bishop was demanding that a more liberal bishop be deposed because of his textual criticism of the Pentateuch. The theological war spread across the British Empire, "The Church's One Foundation" becoming the battle cry for fundamentalists.

In that generation the song fueled division: us versus them. But subsequently the hymn—as condensed by various hymnal editors—has been seen as a symbol of unity; it has called believers from various denominations to quit their bickering, to set aside their differing doctrines and join hands in service, worship, and fellowship that is grounded in the lordship of Christ.

This hymn has taken on particular significance for my colleague Harriet, whose extended family belongs to one denomination, husband to a second, grown daughters to a third and fourth, and herself to a fifth. On one level it is a divided family; on another it is a group deeply committed to "one Lord, one faith, one birth."

In the last year family members were more drastically separated. Harriet's father died. And then her mother—just days after the birth of Harriet's first grandchild. The ensuing tension caused by contradictory emotions—letting go, saying hello—was eased one Sunday morning when Harriet and one of her daughters, worshiping in Harriet's husband's church, sang Stone's memorable last verse: acknowledging the spiritual bond of the body of Christ that transcends death.

> *Yet she on earth hath union with God, the Three in One,*
> *And mystic sweet communion with those whose rest is won.*

Misty-eyed mother and daughter glanced at each other, suddenly relieved of a bit of their grief, feeling not far removed from the watchful saints who've "gone before"—those whom the writer of Hebrews called the heavenly "cloud of witnesses" (12:1).

Consider your own ties to members of the body of Christ who are in some way distanced from you. Maybe you worship in separate buildings or read different Bible translations. Maybe you don't speak the same language theologically—or literally. Still, you can sing to and of the same Lord. Rejoice in your common footing: Jesus, the rock of salvation. Even if you are mourning loved ones who have found their eternal rest, take comfort in the fact that you are mystically bound by Christ, members of one body—and that his waiting bride.

And all this from a pastor's catechism lesson—his fear that parishioners didn't understand the fundamentals of their faith.

Lord, help me to recognize and be willing to learn from fellow members of your church—wherever I find them. May you and that heavenly cloud of witnesses look down on your church and smile—a smile of encouragement as we run the race you see fit to set before us. Not a competitive race, striving against others, but a race run alongside—with and for my brothers and sisters in Christ.

Lift Every Voice and Sing

James Weldon Johnson, 1871 - 1938

Lift every voice and sing
Till earth and heaven ring,
Ring with the harmonies of Liberty. . . .
Sing a song full of the faith that
the dark past has taught us.
Sing a song full of the hope that
the present has brought us. . . .

A few years ago I went with friends—all white—to an outdoor, free concert—the National Symphony Orchestra playing with a colossal choir of nonprofessional musicians culled from church gospel choirs. The evening ended with a rousing rendition of "Lift Every Voice and Sing." And at the first strains of the introduction—with no cue from the conductor—the audience rose to its feet, as if this were Handel's "Hallelujah Chorus."

Well, half the audience. The other half was clueless.

I stood—and with some understanding of why. My friends sat and later seemed surprised when I attempted an explanation.

Let me back up a few more years: I was totally unaware of this song until I was pushing middle age, when I took note of the text in a book by Wanda Jones, wife of Howard Jones, cited as "the first black evangelist on the Billy Graham Crusade staff." Mrs. Jones referred to the lyrics as "the Negro national hymn." But its more common, unofficial, age-old title is a bolder "the Negro national anthem"—and respect for that appellation can bring a crowd to its feet.

As principal of an all-black school in Jacksonville, Florida, James Weldon Johnson wrote the lyrics—and his brother the music (as difficult to sing as "The Star-Spangled Banner")—for a 1900 commemoration of Abraham Lincoln's birthday. The song, which metaphorically recalls a people's painful past in light of a hopeful future, was premiered by a choir of five hundred school children.

"Lift Every Voice" was Johnson's first poem, but not his last. The *World Book Encyclopedia* lists Johnson principally as a poet, but his legacy runs deep and wide: he was the first black lawyer in Florida; later in life he was a diplomat to Venezuela and Nicaragua, and throughout the twenties he was executive secretary of the NAACP, which claimed "Lift Every Voice" as its theme song—then and still.

My friend Rose-Marie—an African American, a few years older than I—recently invited me to dinner. Interested in hymns and looking for "hymn stories," I asked a dumb white question: "You know 'Lift Every Voice and Sing'?"

I repeat. Dumb question.

Here's what I learned: in Harlem in a public school in the fifties, Rose-Marie sang the song once a week in a school assembly—just as I, in upstate New York, sang "My Country 'Tis of Thee."

After dinner she scrounged for an old record album; she wanted me to hear a favorite rendition, sung by Leontyne Price. I listened, touched especially by the last verse:

God of our weary years,
God of our silent tears,
Thou who hast brought us thus far on the way;

> *Thou who hast by thy might,*
> *Led us into the light,*
> *Keep us forever in the path, we pray.*
> *Lest our feet stray from the places,*
>   *our God, where we met thee,*
> *Lest our hearts, drunk with the wine of the world,*
>   *we forget thee;*
> *Shadowed beneath thy hand,*
> *May we forever stand*
> *True to our God,*
> *True to our native land.*

Sitting on her balcony, I realized that this song runs like blood through the veins of a significant portion of my neighbors: the middle-aged and older—if not the young—of African-American descent.

And yet most of my friends do not recognize the tune or the title.

On some level we are clueless. We of them. They of us.

When Johnson finished writing this song, he wept copiously.

And our long generations of racial injustice, disharmony, and misunderstandings make my own heart weep.

What will we do to bridge the breach?

Let's start by claiming the challenge set before the church at Corinth: "God ... reconciled us to himself through Christ and gave us the ministry of reconciliation" (2 Corinthians 5:18).

Lord, make me more sensitive to friends, neighbors, acquaintances, strangers who are different from me in any number of ways— racially, culturally, socially, sexually. Help me listen to them with a respect that plants seeds of reconciliation between that person and myself, between all of us and you.

May the Grace of Christ Our Savior

John Newton, 1725 - 1807

May the grace of Christ our Savior
And the Father's boundless love,
With the Holy Spirit's favor,
Rest upon us from above.

John Newton is best known as the slave-trader who recanted his wretched ways and wrote "Amazing Grace."

But there's more to his story, and it took place years after he left the stormy seas—in midlife, when he was pastor for fifteen years in the small village of Olney, England.

Under his leadership the sleepy Anglican church woke up. Newton reached out and welcomed the town's poor, weavers of bobbin lace. To accommodate the crowds, the church built a balcony. Then Newton convinced the local gentry to open a large manor house to the masses: afternoon religious education for children and evening classes for adults.

For these teaching sessions—and cottage prayer meetings—Newton wrote his own hymns, including "May the Grace of Christ," a benediction suitable for the closing of any gathering.

This isn't just any "God be with you" but the full-orbed trinitarian blessing with which Paul ends his second letter to the Corinthians: "The grace of the Lord Jesus Christ, and the love of God, and the fellowship of the Holy Spirit be with you all" (13:14).

Newton added a second and final verse:

Thus may we abide in union
With each other and the Lord,
And possess, in sweet communion,
Joys which earth cannot afford.

A spirit of community drips from the blessing. May all of God be with all of us. May all of us be with and for each other.

It's a spirit Newton chose to live out, not just write or sing of. We have evidence of this in what we know of Newton's relationship with a troubled and troublesome next-door neighbor, an unemployed lawyer named William Cowper. History remembers Cowper as a poet in his own right, but that distinction is unlikely except for Newton's intercepting grace. (Cowper was chronically depressed and sometimes delusional. See his story as author of "God Moves in a Mysterious Way.")

Albert Edward Bailey describes Newton as Cowper's "good angel." Newton saw Cowper daily, making every attempt to draw the melancholic out of himself and into "gardening, carpentering, a printing press, pets of all kinds ... and finally he proposed that they write together a book of hymns."[2] That book, titled *Olney Hymns,* would take Newton's and Cowper's hymns around the world. It would showcase Cowper's work (which would outstrip Newton's in quality).

Newton knew the critical importance of community. He practiced the art of being there, continually engaging others, looking for ways to bestow blessing. In his later years, after transferring to a parish in London where he pastored until his death at age eighty-two, Newton was known as "Old Good Newton."

He allowed himself to be a messenger of the very benediction he asked his congregation to sing over one another as they parted company. He was willing to be a human instrument of Christ's grace, the Father's love, the Spirit's presence.

May you and I this day reach out to draw someone in to the fellowship of community, granting the favor of the triune God.

May the first "we," the One-but-Three, be with us all, as we go forth to serve with each other, for the Lord.

Lord, we know that Christ prayed that his disciples would be one—in the same way that the Godhead is one. Help me to learn what that means about living in community. Draw me out of myself and allow me to see what I can give to and gain from the brothers and sisters you place around me. Bless us, Lord. Not one but all.

Lord of Our Life

Matthaus von Lowenstern, 1594 – 1648
trans. by Philip Pusey, 1799 – 1855

Lord of our life, and God of our salvation,
Star of our night and hope of every nation,
Hear and receive thy church's supplication,
Lord God Almighty.

This is a hymn born in and for precarious times—when the church in a particular corner of the world felt under siege.

The original German prayer by Matthaus von Lowenstern was written some twenty-five years into Europe's devastating Thirty Years' War—in which Germany lost ten million people. Though originally sparked by royal squabbles, the war was fueled by religious conflicts—Catholics versus Protestants. The church of God in disarray. Lowenstern was pleading God for peace.

Two hundred years later Parliamentarian Philip Pusey discovered Lowenstern's hymn and found it applicable to the state of the church in England. In the nineteenth century the church battles weren't murderous, just angry—and again it was hard to distinguish political and religious issues. The Industrial Revolution was displacing massive numbers of farmworkers—unemployed and homeless. Neither the government nor the state-run church was doing anything to alleviate the suffering. The established church was perceived to be in the hands of wealthy landowners, and it levied unpopular mandatory tithes, in effect, church taxes. Riots broke out. Rifts grew deep. More and more people turned to the "dissenting" churches— Methodist, Baptist, Congregational. Was the kingdom—earthly or heavenly—ever going to recover? When? How? Pusey found comfort in Lowenstern's prayer, which Pusey translated and paraphrased:

> *Hear and receive thy church's supplication. . . .*
>
> *Lord, o'er thy Rock nor death nor hell prevaileth;*
> *Grant us thy peace, Lord:*
> *Peace in our hearts, our evil thoughts assuaging;*
> *Peace in thy church, where brothers are engaging;*
> *Peace, when the world its busy war is waging:*
> *Calm thy foe's raging.*

Parliamentarian Pusey had a clear notion of where God stood politically; he was sure he knew who God's foes were— the discontented dissidents. We may disagree with his perspective, but that does not discount the value and power of his prayer, still relevant in our precarious day: *Lord, hear the prayer of your church; give us peace in our hearts, peace among our brothers and sisters in Christ, peace on earth—if not on earth in our time, then when we rest in heaven.*

"Hear and receive thy church's supplication, Lord God Almighty." It's a timeless prayer.

Of course God receives the solitary prayer of the heart, but Matthew's gospel indicates that there's something about corporate prayer that sets it in a league of its own. Jesus says, "If two of you on earth agree about anything you ask for, it will be done for you by my Father in heaven. For where two or three come together in my name, there am I with them" (Matthew 18:19–20). And when teaching a model prayer, Jesus spoke in the plural: "Our Father. . . . Give us. . . . Forgive us. . . . Lead us . . ." (Matthew 6:9–13).

In recent years, when the church has again been besieged from within and without, many have felt the call to join together in prayer for renewal, for revival, a great awakening. May we all claim Pusey's supplication: Lord, "grant us thy peace."

Lord, remind me of the importance of joining with other believers in a prayer for your blessing on your church.

For All the Saints

William Walsham How, 1823 - 97

For all the saints who from their labors rest,
Who thee by faith before the world confessed,
Thy Name, O Jesus, be forever blessed. Alleluia!

William How's son compared his father to a hymn; his life was "a song of praise to his Creator."

Author of more than fifty hymns, Parson How knew what he liked in the real thing: "A good hymn should be like a good prayer—simple, real, earnest, and reverent." He said nothing about short. Most contemporary hymnals run no more than eight stanzas of his wipeout processional "For All the Saints"; at that they are dropping three of the original eleven ("For the apostles . . . For the evangelists . . . For martyrs . . . ").

Like William How, my friend Dean Liddick knows what *he* likes in a hymn: it should focus on God's sovereignty, majesty, and mercy; acknowledge the importance of human commitment and Christian community; recognize present realities and assure us of God's ultimate triumph. He concludes, "It should communicate a grounded, empowering optimism, not promises of full understanding, prosperity, or even happiness."

And Liddick's chosen "lifetime favorite"? How's processional of praise. Let's return to How's own criteria for a good hymn: "simple, real, earnest, and reverent." Does his work measure up?

Until I sat down to write about this hymn—which never fails to tap some deep well of emotion in my spirit—I would not have called it a simple song. That's probably because How's lyrics have become indelibly identified with the intricate music written for them by Ralph Vaughan Williams.

But simple it is, and for a reason: an Anglican pastor, How wrote this grand sweep to help his uneducated parishioners— a farming village near the border of Wales—get a handle on All Saints' Day (November 1) and the creedal "I believe in . . . the communion of saints."

Each verse is a prayer of three rhymed lines, and the progression is clear: we praise God for the saints gone before who confessed the Lord and looked to him as their strength. May they be our model as we continue their legacy of brave faith until we too rest—and on the last day rise with them, the church triumphant.

Simple, okay. Earnest and reverent, yes. But real? When the song draws us to "a yet more glorious day" when "the countless host" will stream "through gates of pearl"? *Real?* When, unlike the biblical Hebrews 11 commendation of the faithful, How's tribute does not name the saintly—only the God whom they have served? (This point may not have been lost on Vaughn Williams who titled this song's melody, *Sine Nomine:* "Without a Name.")

Yes, real. As real as the legacy of hymn writer How, who eventually became a bishop; he shepherded the church in the slums of East London and later the industrial district of Wakefield—shunning opportunities to serve in more prestigious dioceses. Much loved and respected, How was dubbed "the poor man's bishop" and "the omnibus bishop" because, unlike his peers, he rode public buses, refusing the convenience of a private carriage.

How's song touches a chord because its words ring as true—as real—as our own knowledge of flesh-and-blood heroes of the faith: men and women whose voices and smiles we have known. Authors and artists whose work we have loved. Ancestors whose war stories have become part of our own personal histories. Liddick notes: "Having sung 'For All the Saints' over five decades at the funerals of saints I have known makes it impossible for the words to become abstract. Too many faces. Too many recollections of example. Too many declarations of confidence in their 'Captain in the well-fought fight. . . .'"

Singing of the unnamed "saints who nobly fought" allows us—soldiers still—to pay tribute to our own company of believers.

The dawn of any day can draw us to praise God for all the saints. Named and unnamed. Known and unknown. Here and now. There and gone. Who by faith confessed the Lord, hearing "the distant triumph song," victory to the band—

Singing to Father, Son, and Holy Ghost. Alleluia!

May we thank God for them—and live so that others may thank God for us. May we take a lesson from the apostle Paul who greeted the church at Rome: "To all . . . who are loved by God and called to be saints. . . . First, I thank my God through Jesus Christ for all of you, because your faith is being reported all over the world" (Romans 1:7–8).

*L*ord, *I thank you for the faithful witness of the company of believers—real women and men—who have influenced my own walk of faith. And as I serve you, may others see my life as a song of praise to you: like a good hymn, simple, real, earnest, and reverent. A saint for all seasons.*

Shall We Gather at the River?

Robert Lowry, 1826 - 99

Shall we gather at the river,
Where bright angel feet have trod;
With its crystal tide forever
Flowing by the throne of God?

There's something wonderfully comforting about this song, despite its very present but understated theme: the death of a dear one. The painful departure, the separation, the grief, is a given. It's as obvious as the casket around which everyone stands; it doesn't need to be named but it can't be denied.

Without denying the chasm caused by death, "Shall We Gather at the River?" leaps across it and lands the mourner in a happy heavenly reunion of saints.

Pastor-songwriter Robert Lowry felt particularly inspired to write such a song in the summer of 1864 when he was overwhelmed with the losses at hand. Parishioners and neighbors in Brooklyn, New York, were falling sick, many dying, from a raging "epidemic." And of course the War weighed on everybody's mind.

It was a hot July afternoon. Another death. Another grieving family to console. *Yes, the departed was safe in the arms of Jesus. But that's so far away. The river of death is so wide.*

Sitting at a desk pondering life-and-death issues, Lowry searched his mind looking for musical comfort—and came up short. "Why do hymn writers say so much about the river of death and so little about the pure river of the water of life?" The river described by John the apostle in Revelation 22:1–2: "The angel showed me the river of the water of life, as clear as crystal, flowing from the throne of God and of the Lamb down the middle of the great street of the city."

Lowry's friend and fellow musician Ira Sankey relates the story: "The question began to arise in the heart with unusual emphasis, 'Shall we meet at the river of life?'" Sankey then quotes Lowry, saying, "Seating myself at the parlor organ, simply to give vent to the pent-up emotions of the heart, came the words as if by inspiration."

First the question: "Shall we gather?" And then the decisive answer:

> *Yes, we'll gather at the river,*
> *The beautiful, the beautiful river;*
> *Gather with the saints at the river,*
> *That flows by the throne of God.*

Lowry also "heard" the song's lyrical tune, which perfectly suits the text—the verse melody being mysteriously melancholic, followed by an uplifting refrain.

Even now "Shall We Gather?" is unusual in its emphasis on heaven as a reunion of saints—a picnic in the presence of God.

There's a more "formal" talk of the communion of saints and a distant "cloud" of saintly witnesses who are known to us by reputation only—but a backslapping, bear-hugging heavenly reunion? With family and friends we know and love? Whose presence we have ached for? Cried a creek for?

Lowry lets us imagine yes.

> *There, beside the tranquil river,*
> *Mirror of the Savior's face,*

Happy hearts no more to sever,
Sing of glory and of grace.

Of course heaven is more than a social event. And once we're there, old camaraderies will pale in the presence of the Throne.

On the margin of the river,
Guided by our Shepherd King,
We will walk and worship ever,
His dear footsteps following.

But until then, we can allow ourselves to find comfort in the thought of a riverside reunion. Saint to saint. Friend to friend. Hello, love.

༄

Lord, I thank you for Robert Lowry's glimpse of a heavenly gathering of brothers and sisters. Hope of that meeting makes a devastating death a little easier to bear. Give your saints here on earth the grace to comfort one another when facing loss, especially the death of a loved one.

Part X

Pictures of God

Sometimes a light surprises
The Christian while he sings;
It is the Lord who rises
With healing in his wings.

William Cowper

Guide Me, O Thou Great Jehovah

William Williams, 1717 – 81

Guide me, O thou great Jehovah,
Pilgrim through this barren land;
I am weak, but thou art mighty,
Hold me with thy powerful hand.

For 250 years this hymn has lived up to its early title: "Strength to Pass through the Wilderness."

In her autobiographical book *The White Pagoda,* Fay Angus quotes an uncle, recalling his childhood as the son of missionaries to China at the turn of the last century:

> Great crowds would gather ... to witness executions. We would be on our knees in the living room with my father leading the singing of "Guide me, O thou great Jehovah, pilgrim through this barren land," my mother pedaling for dear life at the harmonium organ, to try and drown out the great shout of "KILL" as the blade descended on the opium–drugged felons.[1]

Go back an additional 150 years and travel halfway around the world, to another wilderness—in Wales, the stomping grounds of itinerant lay preacher William Williams. It was not an easy life. For more than forty years, Williams tramped the countryside, summer or winter—covering more than 90,000 miles on horseback or by foot. And his message hit many young rowdies the wrong way; ruffians repeatedly tormented and attacked Williams, at least once pummeling him to "the verge of Jordan."

And yet Williams also gained a loyal following, maybe because he packaged the gospel in a medium the Welsh loved and understood—music. Affectionately dubbed "the sweet singer of Wales," he wrote some eight hundred hymns, many quickly memorized by country folk who had never learned to read. Of those songs only "Guide Me, O Thou Great Jehovah" remains popular to this day.

I like that old tag line: "Strength to Pass through the Wilderness." Phrase after phrase of Williams's hymn recounts God's provision for the children of Israel—Moses and his pilgrims—through a barren land. Manna from heaven. Water from a rock. God's guiding presence evident as a cloud by day, a fire by night.

The Exodus story reduced to three verses does fortify faith—even for those of us who, if we are honest, admit that we know nothing about life in the real wilderness.

Drowning out death chants.

Huddling in dirty ditches.

Forty years on horseback, harassed.

Forty years eating manna—"what-is-it?" dust off the desert floor.

But we all know something of being weak, feeling vulnerable. We all have known at least a hint of hunger and the delight of being utterly satisfied. We are able to leap from the physical to the spiritual realm and understand the poet's plea: "Bread of heaven, Bread of heaven, / Feed me till I want no more."

Walking out of a wilderness of his own, Jesus talked about one's spiritual sustenance in terms of bread. Still starved from a forty-day fast, he said, "Man does not live on bread alone" (Matthew 4:4).

Months later, after feeding five thousand from a picnic basket, he confronted some greedy groupies looking for another miraculous free lunch. They had it all wrong, Jesus said. He talked at some length, discussing Moses and manna and finally hitting the bottom line of wilderness training: "I am the living bread that came down from heaven. . . . Your forefathers ate manna and died, but he who feeds on this bread will live forever" (John 6:51, 58).

Christ himself is our sustenance on the journey through this barren land. You only need to reach out to accept the daily provision. Strength to pass through the wilderness. Take and eat of the Bread of Life.

Lord, I reach out to receive the spiritual food you offer me. Feed me till I want no more. Feed me now and evermore.

Like as a Mother Comforteth

William Runyan, 1870 – 1957

"Like as a mother comforteth"—
O words of gentle worth!
"So will I comfort you," declares
The Lord of all the earth.

In these pages I have tried to stay away from the obscure—lyrics that never gained much of an audience either among circles that favor subjective gospel songs or in churches preferring more formal worship hymns.

But one hymn buried in the denominational hymnbook of my childhood keeps demanding a hearing. It's sung to the familiar tune used for "O for a Closer Walk with God," and its first verse is pulled straight from the prophet's "thus saith the Lord": "As a mother comforts her child, / so will I comfort you" (Isaiah 66:13).

I'm glad this song made its way into my personal repertoire. But I have questions: Did we sing it—like "Faith of Our Mothers"—only once a year, on Mother's Day? Why is it stuck in the back of the hymnal under a "Home" heading and not in the mainstream of "Assurance" or maybe "Peace and Contentment"? Why can't I find it in any other hymnbooks?

Its author William Runyan was not a nobody. He wrote the melody of "Great Is Thy Faithfulness." He wrote the tune and lyrics for the prayerful "Lord, I Have Shut the Door." Before retiring he was associated with a major hymnal publisher and Moody Bible Institute.

When it comes to hymnbooks, I don't claim to know why certain songs "make the cut" while others are left behind. It's not a question I've even thought about—until I went hunting for this personal favorite. And couldn't find it. The question niggled: Is it ignored because of our discomfort with feminine images of God? Are we so focused on the sanctity of "the fatherhood of God" that we choose to ignore the biblical images that show our God—a Being beyond gender, a Spirit who dwells in a realm beyond genitalia—as having motherly or feminine qualities?

A lovely devotional book written by Sarah Hornsby has sold well for more than a decade; *At the Name of Jesus* includes 365 daily readings, each centered on an Old or New Testament name of Jesus. Understandably, many of her choices are masculine, including Father, Husband, Son. Some of her names are obscure and obviously analogical: "Jesus is the Dew," based on Hosea 14:5: "I will be like the dew to Israel"; "Jesus is the Olive Tree," based on Hosea 14:6, "His beauty will be like an olive tree" (NASB); "Jesus is the Pearl of great price," based on Matthew 13:45–46. Not one of these 365 names is blatantly feminine—no "hen" (Matthew 23:37); no "eagle" bearing her young (Exodus 19:4); no "she-bear" (Hosea 13:8); no "comforting mother" from Isaiah.[2]

Maybe it's time to think about the challenge presented in the title of J. B. Phillips's classic *Your God Is Too Small*.

In *Death Comes for the Archbishop,* Willa Cather describes her main character as being "much greater than the sum of his qualities." A thoughtful description that might be used of the One-in-Three I AM. Much greater than the sum of the divine qualities. Much greater than the sum of the deific names, descriptions, and poetic images we have at our disposal.

Maybe it's time to resurrect a great old song as a reminder of an Old Testament image of God. Not to replace "Dear Lord and Father of Mankind" but to round out the picture.

> *"Like as a mother"—grant, O God,*
> *This likeness e'er may be*
> *A holy symbol to declare*
> *This love that dwells in thee.*

Lord, do not allow me to close my eyes to the truth of who you are. As I look to your Word for clarity, show me more facets of your being—beyond the confines of my limited understanding.

The Light of the World Is Jesus

Philip Bliss, 1838 – 76

The whole world was lost in the darkness of sin;
The Light of the world is Jesus. . . .

Philip Bliss wrote this song the year before he died, his short life dramatically snuffed out in a noble but unsuccessful attempt to save his wife from a fiery train derailment.

It seems the song itself had no comparably dramatic inception. Bliss's evangelist colleague and biographer Major D. W. Whittle noted that "The Light of the World" was written at Bliss's home. It "came to him all together, words and music, one morning while passing through the hall to his room, and was at once written out."

In his classic *One Hundred and One Hymn Stories*, Carl Price gives a moving account, not of the writing of this song but about its testimony and meaning.

The tale is about Dr. S. Earl Taylor, missionary secretary of the Methodist Episcopal Church sometime near the turn of the last century. Taylor was visiting Calcutta just preceding and during a solar eclipse. Among the Indian people he noted "a superstitious dread of an eclipse of the sun. They fear that the sun is being swallowed by a demon of some sort." Price continues:

For days before that event [Taylor] saw the city's
streets crowded with pilgrims on their way to various
sacred places, where they hoped to worship and bathe in
the Hooghly River just below the Ganges during the time
of the eclipse, expecting thereby to ward off evil. When at
last the fateful hour of darkness arrived hundreds of thousands of natives thronged the sacred waters, terrorized by
the eclipse and making a great clamor because they feared
that a great power of evil in the form of a snake was about
to swallow the sungod. As Dr. Taylor, looking from the
YMCA Building, witnessed this . . . he heard a group of
native Christians singing in their meeting:

> *The whole world was lost in the darkness of sin;*
> *The Light of the world is Jesus.*[3]

Price concludes by reflecting on the spiritual darkness
caused by "the eclipse of Jesus." The light shines but sometimes
our view is blocked. Verse 3 of Bliss's song speaks in terms of a
more personal obstruction—spiritual cataracts:

> *Ye dwellers in darkness with sin-blinded eyes,*
> *The Light of the world is Jesus. . . .*

> *Come to the Light, 'tis shining for thee;*
> *Sweetly the Light has dawned upon me;*
> *Once I was blind, but now I can see;*
> *The Light of the world is Jesus.*

The apostle John repeatedly refers to Jesus in terms of
light: "God is light; in him there is no darkness at all" (1 John
1:5). In his gospel John quotes Jesus, saying, "I am the light of
the world" (John 8:12).

John also repeatedly calls Jesus' followers to *walk* in the
light of Christ—with cataracts removed, with vision clear.
"Whoever follows me will never walk in darkness, but will
have the light of life" (John 8:12).

In *Readings in St. John's Gospel,* William Temple, archbishop of Canterbury during World War II, proffers an explanation of how this works: "Christ the Light of the World shines first upon the soul, and then from within the soul upon the path of life. He does not illumine our way while leaving us unconverted; but by converting us He illumines our way."[4]

Removes the obstructions. Lets the sun shine in, the sunshine in.

Lord, in you there is no darkness at all. I know that and yet some days my view—of who you are, of who I am, of who my neighbors are—is particularly cloudy, even eclipsed. Open my eyes. Illumine my path. Help me to see the light and then walk in it.

What a Friend We Have in Jesus

Joseph Scriven, 1820 – 86

What a friend we have in Jesus,
All our sins and griefs to bear!

This is a song for the lonely—those who ever have been, are, or will be—written by a man who was familiar with friendship and acquainted with grief. Various threads of his life story—the tragedy, the mercy, the mystery—bear retelling.

After graduating from Trinity College in Dublin and spending several years in a military college, Joseph Scriven was forced by poor health to switch careers. Taking up theology, he studied for the Anglican ministry, though in time he decided not to "go for" ordination.

Then, the night before Scriven was to be married, his bride was thrown from a horse—into the river in which she drowned.

Some say Scriven never quite recovered from this loss. At the age of twenty-five he left Ireland—alone—for Canada, where he was a family tutor on Rice Lake in Ontario. There Scriven fell in love again, but alas tragedy struck twice: his fiancée died of pneumonia, shortly after being baptized in the biting cold lake.

It seems that Scriven wrote "What a Friend" at this juncture—in 1855, for his mother, possibly sending it to her with the news of his misfortune and grief. (Can a mother bear her son's sorrow?) One copy he mailed to Ireland. Another—of draft manuscript quality and titled "Pray without Ceasing"— went into his own scrapbook. It's not at all clear how the poem—with no author attribution at all—found its way into an 1865 book published in Boston: *Social Hymns, Original and Selected*. Ten years later Ira Sankey made a last minute substitution to include it in a widely distributed gospel-song collection. He later noted that "the last hymn that went into the book became one of the first in favor."

Scriven never did marry. He was increasingly viewed as an eccentric—sometimes tormented by town toughs. But if eccentric, the element was entwined with a faith that worked. He was known for "preaching to everyone about the love of Jesus." There was nothing empty about his words; a friend to the needy, he went about doing good, for example, sawing wood for the sick and the widows too poor to hire help. (It's said he would be "handyman" *only* for people who couldn't pay for his services.) When he saw a need, he gave people money (not that he had much), his own winter clothing, his time. After Scriven's death a liquor salesman in town said, "If ever there was a saint on earth, it was Joseph Scriven."

Never robust, Scriven's health failed him before he reached nature's allotted three-score years and ten. Hearing of his predicament, friends took him in. Thumbing through Scriven's scrapbooks, his host-nurse, a Mr. Sackville, found an old handwritten copy of the popular song. The wheels began churning. "Did you write this?" he asked.

For my mother, he explained. *I didn't intend anyone else to see it.*

When asked again—directly—if he'd written the poem, Scriven answered, "The Lord and I did it between us."[†]

This one statement makes me think this man knew the friendship of Christ as well as he knew grief. To Scriven, Christ was a present partner, a burden bearer, helpmate who came alongside to inspire, to encourage, and help carry the load. "Can we find a friend so faithful / Who will all our sorrows share?" This is the type of friend noted in Proverbs 18:24, "who sticks closer than a brother." This is *the* Friend who "took up our infirmities / and carried our sorrows" (Isaiah 53:4).[†]

And Jesus is *the* Friend who remains steady, still today. When we're lonely, feeling abandoned, in need of a soul mate. Jesus' word to his disciples might be his word to us: "I no longer call you servants, because a servant does not know his master's business. Instead, I have called you friends" (John 15:15).

*L*ord, *allow me to know you as the friend who sticks closer than a brother.*

[†]I might end the story there, but Scriven's death is shrouded with such mystery that I cannot cut short the account. October 9–10, 1886: Scriven was sick, feverish, possibly delirious. He was also by some accounts severely depressed over his deteriorating health and his inability to care for himself, physically and financially. Some postulate that he was still haunted by the loss of his first love, river-swept from his life. With what intent or purpose, no one knows, but sometime in the night he left his bed. In the morning he was found down by the lake, on his knees as if in prayer, his forehead to the ground—drowned in six shallow inches of water.

God Moves in a Mysterious Way

William Cowper, 1731 – 1800

friends w/
John Newton

God moves in a mysterious way
His wonders to perform;
He plants his footsteps in the sea
And rides upon the storm.

When this song was published, about five years after it was written, William Cowper and his copublisher/neighbor/infinitely-patient-friend John Newton (author of "Amazing Grace") titled it "Light Shining out of Darkness." Maybe it should have been "Sanity Shining out of Senility."

"William Cowper's poetry was the sanest thing about him," quips Virginia Stem Owens.[5] Call his malady melancholia or bipolar depression, either way the man lived an emotionally tortured life. As a young lawyer panicked at the prospects of a particular job interview, he plotted suicide. Three attempts mysteriously failed: "paralyzed" hands refusing to lift a poisoned potion, a knife breaking at the critical moment, a garter snapping when tested by Cowper's hanging weight.

Subsequently pulled taut by guilt, *he* snapped. In an asylum months later he made peace with God, a peace that sustained him for about ten years before another dark cloud descended, in 1773. Described by friends as being "almost an infant," Cowper heard voices, saw visions, imagined scheming enemies, and personalized God's wrath. He again tried to kill himself, this time convinced it was God's will: as God had asked Abraham to give up Isaac, God was asking him to end his life— to hasten his damnation.

Friends foiled his suicide attempts, and within a year Cowper regained some modicum of normalcy (the insanity would return), going on to write secular poetry that placed him among the greats of his day.

"God Moves in a Mysterious Way" is somehow linked to the madness of 1773. Some sources postulate it was written after he'd regained his senses. Others speculate the verse was penned as he was planning his final exit.

Several years later, Cowper or Newton had the presence of mind to tag this poem "Light Shining out of Darkness." I choose to believe this is an oblique reference to John 1:5: "The light shineth in darkness; and the darkness comprehended it not" (KJV).

Last week a twenty-five-year-old woman struggling to find her career niche phoned her father, a theology professor. She'd come oh-so-close to getting The Perfect Job, which ultimately had gone to Someone Else. Her question, asked with a quavering voice: "Isn't there a verse that says if God's children ask for bread, he won't give them a stone?"

The dad knew the reference. "That's the gist of part of the Sermon on the Mount, Matthew 7. If earthly parents will provide bread and eggs, not stones and scorpions, 'how much more will your Father in heaven give good gifts to those who ask him.' Why the question?"

"Well, Dad, what do you do when you ask for bread and God gives you a stone?"

The professor groaned with the weight of his daughter's pain. He groped for words, wanting to bolster her faith without spewing platitudes.

When the father relayed the conversation to me, I thought of Cowper's song.

Judge not the Lord by feeble sense,
But trust him for his grace;
Behind a frowning providence
He hides a smiling face.

And then I thought of Cowper, who spent most of his life hoping—but not assuredly *feeling*—that the Lord's face was shining upon him.

And I wanted to wrap the professor's daughter in my arms and urge her to open her eyes to the light that shines in and out of the darkness—though sometimes it can be seen only through the lens of the mad poet, who concluded the song:

God is his own interpreter,
And he will make it plain.

*L*ord, sometimes I ask for bread and I'm sure you give me a stone. I just don't understand what you're up to and why. *Increase my faith. Forgive my blind unbelief. Reach down through the mystery as I reach up for your love.*

At the Name of Jesus

Caroline Maria Noel, 1817 - 77

At the Name of Jesus
Every knee shall bow,
Every tongue confess him
King of glory now;
'Tis the Father's pleasure
We should call him Lord,
Who from the beginning
Was the mighty Word.

I started this book last spring at an informal retreat—a few women gathering off-season at Rehoboth Beach, Delaware, for spiritual renewal.

With the same group I returned a year later, finished manuscript in hand. I would read it through—make a few minor adjustments—before sending it off to the publisher. As I sat on the beach mulling over my work, I regretted not having included only one song: "At the Name of Jesus" by Caroline Noel. Thanks to its throne-room tune by Ralph Vaughan Williams, it's a favorite of many and mine. It had been sung at a friend's ordination. I had found a little but not much information about Noel. Like many other nineteenth-century female hymn writers, she never married. She wrote a few hymns as a teenager and then none until age forty, when her health failed. She wrote this lengthy hymn as an Ascension Day processional, expanding a Pauline passage in Philippians 2. The Amplified Bible reads: "That in (at) the name of Jesus every knee should (must) bow, in heaven and on earth and under the earth, And every tongue [frankly and openly] confess and acknowledge that Jesus Christ is Lord, to the glory of God the Father" (vv. 10–11).[†] But a favored-hymn status buttressed by such slight background information wasn't inspiration enough for me to write a reflection.

Such were my regrets as I sat at the beach last week—on Ascension Day—when I was interrupted by a fellow retreatant. "Would you like to go for a walk?" she asked.

Not exactly what I had in mind. But sensing I needed to be less bookish, I smiled and said sure—let's. Was I surprised at the next hour's conversation!

She wanted to tell me what had happened to her here, at the beach, last spring. By the power of—in the name of—Jesus, she'd been released from years of demonic nightmares and suicidal obsessions. A darkness had lifted; she'd been healed. Her story explained the lightness, even brightness I'd noticed recently in her face and demeanor.

I thought that was the end of the story. There was more. Though she'd always been a spiritual person, she'd long ago discarded any notion that Jesus offered anything above and beyond other acclaimed religious leaders. Any such claims could be chalked up to ignorance—or arrogance.

But the night after her healing, sitting beside her spiritual mentor on the Rehoboth boardwalk, she'd looked out over the Atlantic and caught a glimpse of eternity. In a vision, she'd seen the horizon open up. "I saw Jesus—standing on the right—

[†]The parenthetical explanations, giving nuances of the original language, are an integral part of the Amplified Bible.

reigning in glory. And in waves—like a circular farm combine—I saw everyone who had ever been born and ever would be born. I saw Confucius, Buddha. Everyone. Millions. All centuries flashed by. And every person acknowledged that Jesus was Lord. Jesus stood apart, outside of the limits of time, eternal. Suddenly it was so obvious: What he had done—his incarnation, death, and resurrection—was once and for all. He wasn't one among many holy seers. He was—is—the Son of God, and he will come again when everyone has had the chance to hear his name."

I listened, amazed at what she'd seen where the ocean—the earth—met the sky. When her story wound to a close, I asked her if she knew Noel's song, "At the name of Jesus every knee shall bow."

She didn't. Later we found a hymnal and sang the long narrative: Jesus conquered death and then he

> *Bore [his lordship] up triumphant*
> > *With its human light,*
> *Through all ranks of creatures,*
> > *To the central height,*
> *To the throne of Godhead,*
> > *To the Father's breast. . . .*

We sang down to the last verse. She looked up at me, amazed, her eyes filled with tears: "That's what I saw! This is it."

My manuscript wasn't finished—not without this closing picture of Jesus, enthroned in glory. He whose name is above every name:

> *He is God the Savior,*
> > *He is Christ the Lord,*
> *Ever to be worshiped,*
> > *Trusted, and adored.*

And our story isn't finished because

. . . *this Lord Jesus*
Shall return again,
With his Father's glory,
With his angel Train;
For all wreaths of empire
Meet upon his brow,
And our hearts confess him
King of glory now.

O come let us adore him, this Christ, our Lord.

Lord, I cannot grasp the grandeur of who you are. And yet I praise you—through all times and all names, you are the same—Jesus the Lord.

Softly and Tenderly, Jesus Is Calling

Will L. Thompson, 1847 – 1909

Softly and tenderly, Jesus is calling,
Calling for you and for me;
See on the portals he's waiting and watching,
Watching for you and for me.

Come home.

Our hymnbooks are full of invitations.

Sometimes the songs request that God come to us. Sometimes they bid us to come home to him.

Written in 1880 by Will Thompson, an Ohio music-store owner and music publisher, this soft and tender invitation became a favorite at turn-of-the-century revivals.

Nineteen years after the song's publication, Thompson visited a dying Dwight L. Moody—the premiere, nationally renowned evangelist of his day. Though visitors were restricted, Moody insisted that Thompson be allowed to come in. A reflective Moody, looking back over his persuasive ministry, his crowd-drawing preaching, gave Thompson the ultimate compliment: "I would rather have written 'Softly and Tenderly,' than anything I have been able to do in my whole life."

Thompson's song tugs at the heart.

> *Come home, come home,*
> *Ye who are weary, come home.*
> *Earnestly, tenderly, Jesus is calling,*
> *Calling, O sinner, come home.*

Another notable in Moody's circle of friends, gospel songwriter Fanny Crosby, once nudged a New York "Bowery bum" toward the Kingdom, piquing his interest by noting that "the sweetest words in our language or any other are *mother, home,* and *heaven.*"

Come home. The invitation works for the dying: The choir of Atlanta's Ebenezer Baptist Church sang Thompson's classic at Martin Luther King's memorial service.

> *Time is now fleeting; the moments are passing . . .*
> *Shadows are gathering; deathbeds are coming,*
> *Coming for you and for me.*
> *Come home. Come home.*

It works for the homesick. Cynthia Clawson's interpretation of the song winds hauntingly through the 1985 movie *Trip to Bountiful,* the story of an old woman's obsession: to escape Houston and her ditzy daughter-in-law and get back to her homestead in Bountiful, Texas. (I think of the William Wordsworth lines: "Homeless near a thousand homes I stood, / And near a thousand tables pined and wanted food.")

It works for the wayfaring. My colleague Peggy says she came to Christ, being drawn by Thompson's music as rendered in the *Bountiful* movie, which is ultimately a woman's journey to freedom. Not freedom from a daughter-in-law but freedom of spirit. Peggy recalls watching the movie when it was broadcast on TV.

> It was one of those serendipitous events. I turned
> on the TV and there were two women riding on a bus,
> talking. Believe it or not, the scene was compelling. Then

came the song: "Softly and tenderly Jesus is calling. / See on the portals he's waiting and watching, / Watching for you and for me." The image flashed into my mind of Jesus standing on a rock beckoning me with soft and loving eyes. He was motioning to me with his right arm to come to him. He could not understand why I would not come and accept this love that was waiting, just for me.

For weeks afterward I sang that song and tried to learn the words. I sang and cried while I did the dishes. I sang and cried while I folded the clothes. One day my husband started singing along. Startled, I asked him how he knew the words. He said it was an old hymn they sang in all the Baptist churches. (I had never heard it in a Catholic church.) I was amazed—right here in my own home was someone who could teach the words to me. "How could you know this song and not sing it or share it?" I demanded. To him it was just another hymn among many. To me it evoked a personal call from Jesus to me to open my heart to him. It was the most beautiful music in the world:

> *O for the wonderful love he has promised . . .*
> *Though we have sinned, he has mercy and pardon,*
> *Pardon for you and for me.*
> *Come home. Come home.*

Fanny Crosby placed *home* among the most beautiful words in any language. And poet Wordsworth pictured God as being "our home."

Home, where the porch light is always on, beckoning. Not understanding why any homesick child would not come all the way in.

> *If you make the Most High your dwelling . . .*
> *then no harm will befall you,*
> *no disaster will come near your tent.*

Psalm 91:9 - 10

Lord, I have come to you as my home. And yet I know that you are always beckoning me further in. I open myself to you today. I hear your call to come home, past the parlor, into the kitchen to sit at your table.

Notes

Introduction

    1. Dale Brown, "A Conversation with Garrison Keillor, " *Image* 9 (1995), 49.

    2. Mary Gordon, "My Mother Is Speaking from the Desert, " *New York Times Magazine* (March 19, 1995), 48.

    3. Nelle Vander Ark, "A Song of Trust," *Perspectives* (November 1996), 18.

Part I: Gifts of God

    1. Sharon Olds, "The Prayer," in *The Gold Cell* (New York: Knopf, 1987), 77.

    2. Ian Bradley, *The Book of Hymns* (Woodstock, N.Y.: Overlook Press, 1989), 447.

Part II: Tidings of Christmas Joy

    1. Mary McGrory, "Snow, Plows and Power," *Washington Post* (11 January 1996), 2.

    2. Percy Dearmer, Ralph Vaughan Williams, and Martin Shaw, *The Oxford Book of Carols* (London: Oxford University Press, 1928), v.

Part III: Psalms in Songs

    1. Christopher Idle, *Stories of Our Favorite Hymns* (Grand Rapids: Eerdmans, 1980), 15.

    2. Albert Edward Bailey, *The Gospel in Hymns* (New York: Charles Scribner's, 1950), 17, 25.

3. Albert Christ-Janer, Charles Hughes, and Carleton Sprague-Smith, *American Hymns Old and New* (New York: Columbia University Press, 1980), 294–95.

Part IV: Lines Learned as Children

1. Janet LindeBladJanzen and Richard Foster, *Songs for Renewal* (San Francisco: HarperCollins, 1995), 9.

2. Eugene Peterson, "The Pastor's Sabbath," *Leadership* (Spring 1985), 53, as quoted in Marva Dawn, *Keeping the Sabbath Wholly* (Grand Rapids: Eerdmans, 1989), 58.

3. C. Stephen Evans, "Can the New Jesus Save Us?" *Books and Culture* (November-December 1995), 8.

4. Quoted in John Bartlett, ed., *Familiar Quotations,* 15th ed. (Boston: Little, Brown, 1980), 837.

5. Cecilia Margaret Rudin, *Stories of Hymns We Love* (Chicago: John Rudin, 1934), 87.

Part V: Lessons from the Gospels

1. Tawnia Wheeler, "If Not for You," *Jubilee* (April 1995), 1–3. Used by permission of Prison Fellowship, P.O. Box 17500, Washington, DC 20041.

2. Gail Ramshaw, *Words That Sing* (Chicago: Archdiocese of Chicago, Liturgy Training Publications, 1992), 117.

Part VI: Words That Challenge

1. Richard Mouw, "A Kinder, Gentler Calvinism," *Reformed Journal* (October 1990), 13. Used by permission of the author.

2. William Reynolds, *Songs of Glory* (Grand Rapids: Zondervan, 1990), 104.

3. Martin Luther King, Jr., *I Have a Dream: Writings and Speeches That Changed the World,* ed. James M. Washington (San Francisco: HarperCollins, 1992), 203.

4. Tim Stafford, "Why Volunteers Won't Save America," *Christianity Today* (29 April 1996), 23.

Part VII: Hymns as Prayers

1. George Beverly Shea, *Then Sings My Soul* (Grand Rapids: Revell, 1968), 145.

Part VIII: Songs of Testimony

1. Albert Edward Bailey, *The Gospel in Hymns* (New York: Charles Scribner's, 1950), 175. Bailey acknowledges the paragraph is condensed from Bowring's original. Ellipses indicate my further condensation.

2. Evelyn Bence, *Leaving Home* (Philadelphia: Westminster Press, 1982).

Part IX: Celebration of Community

1. J. B. Phillips, *The Newborn Christian* (New York: Macmillan, 1978), 144.

2. Albert Edward Bailey, *The Gospel in Hymns* (New York: Charles Scribner's, 1950), 131.

Part X: Pictures of God

1. Fay Angus, *The White Pagoda* (Wheaton, Ill.: Tyndale, 1978), 27.

2. Sarah Hornsby, *At the Name of Jesus* (Grand Rapids: Chosen Books, 1983).

3. Carl Price, *One Hundred and One Hymn Stories* (Nashville: Abingdon, 1923), 20.

4. Quoted in William Sykes, ed., *Visions of Faith* (Basingstoke, Hants, England: Marshall Pickering, 1986), 201.

5. Virginia Stem Owens, "William Cowper, Crazy Christian," *Perspectives* (April 1993), 13.

ℬibliography

Bailey, Albert Edward. *The Gospel in Hymns.* New York: Charles Scribner's, 1950.

Barrows, Cliff, et al. *Crusader Hymns and Hymn Stories.* Minneapolis: Billy Graham Evangelistic Association, Hope Publishing, 1966, 1967.

Blanchard, Kathleen. *Stories of Popular Hymns.* Grand Rapids: Zondervan, 1939.

_____. *Stories of Favorite Hymns.* Grand Rapids: Zondervan, 1940.

_____. *Stories of Beautiful Hymns.* Grand Rapids: Zondervan, 1942.

Bradley, Ian. *The Book of Hymns.* Woodstock, N.Y.: Overlook Press, 1989.

Christ-Janer, Albert, Charles Hughes, and Carleton Sprague-Smith. *American Hymns Old and New.* New York: Columbia University Press, 1980.

Clark, Elmer T. *Charles Wesley: The Singer of the Evangelical Revival.* Nashville: The Upper Room, 1957.

Companion to the Hymnal. Nashville: Abingdon, 1970.

Dearmer, Percy, Ralph Vaughan Williams, and Martin Shaw. *The Oxford Book of Carols.* London: Oxford University Press, 1928.

Dough, Whitney. *Our Unknown Friends: The Hymn Writers.* Orlando: Messages, 1983.

Enock, Esther. *Memoirs of Mighty Men and Women: Frances Ridley Havergal*. London: Pickering & Inglis, nd.

Harvey, Robert. *Best-Loved Hymn Stories*. Grand Rapids: Zondervan, 1963.

Hustad, Donald P. *Jubilate II*. Carol Stream, Ill.: Hope Publishing, 1993.

Idle, Christopher. *Stories of Our Favorite Hymns*. Grand Rapids: Eerdmans, 1980.

Janzen, Janet Lindeblad with Richard Foster. *Songs for Renewal*. San Francisco: HarperCollins, 1995.

Konkle, Wilbur. *Living Hymn Stories*. Minneapolis: Bethany Fellowship, 1971.

Parry, Kenneth. *Christian Hymns*. Chicago: SCM Book Club, 1956.

Peters, Erskine. *Lyrics of the Afro-American Spiritual*. Westport, Conn.: Greenwood Press, 1993.

Price, Carl. *One Hundred and One Hymn Stories*. Nashville: Abingdon, 1923.

_____. *More Hymn Stories*. Nashville: Abingdon, 1929.

Ramshaw, Gail. *Words That Sing*. Chicago: Archdiocese of Chicago, Liturgy Training Publications, 1992.

Reynolds, William. *Hymns of Our Faith*. Nashville: Broadman, 1964.

_____. *Songs of Glory*. Grand Rapids: Zondervan, 1990.

Rudin, Cecelia Margaret. *Stories of Hymns We Love*. Chicago: John Rudin, 1934, 1951.

Ruffin, Bernard. *Fanny Crosby*. New York: Pilgrim Press, United Church Press, 1976.

Shea, George Beverly. *Then Sings My Soul*. Grand Rapids: Fleming H. Revell, 1968.

Terry, Lindsay. *Devotionals from Famous Hymn Stories*. Grand Rapids: Baker, 1974, 1986.